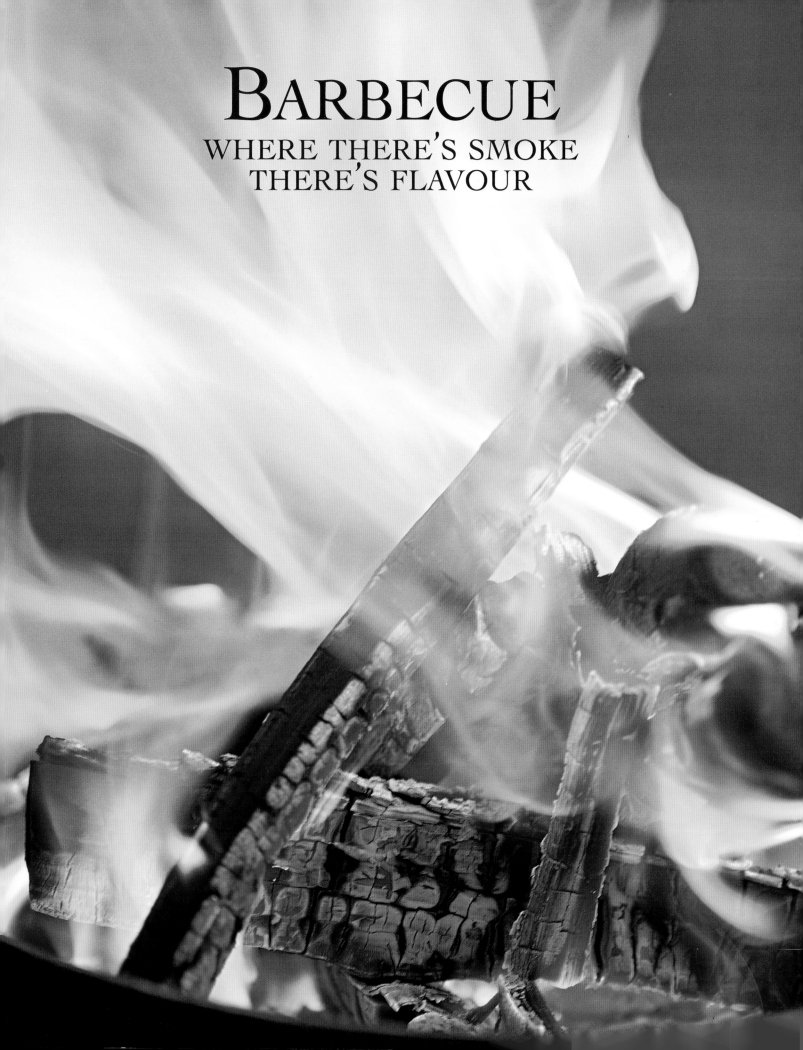

BARBECUE
WHERE THERE'S SMOKE THERE'S FLAVOUR

BARBECUE
WHERE THERE'S SMOKE THERE'S FLAVOUR

Eric Treuillé & Birgit Erath

Photography by
IAN O'LEARY

A Dorling Kindersley Book

Dorling Kindersley

LONDON, NEW YORK, SYDNEY, DELHI, PARIS,
MUNICH and JOHANNESBURG

EDITORIAL CONSULTANT
Rosie Kindersley

DESIGN AND ART DIRECTION
Stuart Jackman

PROJECT EDITOR
Julia Pemberton Hellums

EDITOR
Sally Somers

PRODUCTION CONTROLLER
Elizabeth Cherry

FOOD STYLING
Eric Treuillé

DEDICATION
*To our families, in London,
Germany and France, in fond
memory of much outdoor feasting.*

2 4 6 8 10 9 7 5 3

First published in Great Britain in 2000 by
Dorling Kindersley Limited,
9 Henrietta Street, London WC2E 8PS

A CIP catalogue record for this book is available from the British Library

Hardback ISBN 0 7513 2719 0

Colour reproduction in Italy by GRB
Printed and bound by Graficas Estella, Spain

for our complete
catalogue visit
www.dk.com

CONTENTS

INTRODUCTION

All around the world people cook over open fire. It's how cooking began and it has stood the test of time. It's today's favourite way to cook and it is easy to understand why. Grilling means no fuss, less fat, more flavour, most fun. Nothing brings out the best flavour in food quite like eating it sizzling hot off the barbecue grill.

Good food means a good time, and a gathering around the barbie makes any meal a celebration. Friends and family mix, mingle and unwind as steaks sear and ribs sizzle. Casual, yet a real occasion, a barbecue party sets appetites on fire.

There's something elemental about open-fire cooking. Could it be that those dancing flames, glowing embers and smoky aromas awaken our long-lost primordial selves?

Even people with the most hard-boiled "I can't cook" attitudes are unable to resist the excitement of cooking over coals.

We don't want to get too serious, because, to us, grilling isn't serious. This book is not a heavy-weight volume crammed with everything you need to know to grill like a pro. It's about having fun outdoors with food, flavour and fire.

Grilling shouldn't mean burnt steak, scorched chicken and other charred remains. Say goodbye to all that. Say hello to great grilled food every time. We've identified the key factors to guarantee grilling success, and we've made them simple.

To make our recipes, all you need are a few ingredients, hot coals and a sense of adventure. So relax. Just do it. Because we all love food hot off the grill. Come outside and join the party!

Eric Biguet

NOTES FROM THE COOKS

BEFORE YOU COOK read through the recipe carefully. Make sure you have all the equipment and ingredients required. In all recipes, vegetables are washed and peeled, unless otherwise stated.

ON PREHEATING

We have given instructions for indoor as well as outdoor grilling. But, whether grilling outdoors or indoors, be sure to allow enough time to get your grill up to the desired firepower. Successful grilling must sear the surface of food quickly to form a flavourful crust and to seal the succulent juices inside. Inadequate preheating means the crust does not form, the juices leak out, and you have uniformly tough, dry and tasteless results.

For charcoal barbecue grills, light up 30-40 minutes before you want to start grilling. This gives the coals time to reach the perfect temperature for a hot fire.

For gas barbecue grills, allow 10-15 minutes to preheat the lava rocks to the desired temperature.

For ridged cast iron grill pans, set over a medium high heat 3 minutes before grilling. To see if it is hot enough, splash a few drops of water on the surface: they should sizzle and evaporate immediately.

For overhead grills, allow 5-10 minutes to preheat an electric overhead grill and 3-5 minutes for a gas grill before you want to start.

ON TASTING

Always taste food as you cook and before you serve. Don't be afraid to add or change flavours to suit your palate - the fun of cooking is in experimenting, improvising, creating. Ingredients differ from day to day, season to season and kitchen to kitchen. Be prepared to adjust sweetness, sharpness, spiciness, and, most important of all, salt, to your own taste. The amount of salt and pepper used to season food makes the difference between good and great food.

SALT AND PEPPER

As a general guideline, allow 2 tsp salt and 1 tsp pepper for every 4 servings of meat. In practice, ingredients vary, palates vary and even salts vary, but this remains a good guideline.

ON MEASURING

Accurate measurements are essential if you want the same good results each time you follow a recipe. We have given measurements in metric and imperial in all the recipes. Always stick to one set of measurements. Never use a mixture of both in the same recipe.

Kitchen scales are the most accurate way to measure dry ingredients. We recommend using scales for all except the smallest amounts.

We recommend using cooks' measuring spoons when following a recipe. All spoon measurements in the book are level unless otherwise stated. To measure dry ingredients with a spoon, scoop the ingredient lightly from the storage container, then level the surface with the edge of a straight-bladed knife.

We use standard level spoon measurements:
    1 tbsp - 15ml (½ floz)
    1 tsp - 5ml (⅙ floz)

To measure liquids, choose a transparent glass or plastic measuring jug. Always place the jug on a flat surface and check for accuracy at eye level when pouring in a liquid to measure.

A final and important rule of measuring - never measure ingredients over the mixing bowl!

THE GRILL

THE BASIC EQUIPMENT

All you need is a fire, some food and a rack, so that the food doesn't actually end up in the fire. That's it. Anything from the latest, state-of-the-art model of barbecue grill to a simple set-up of a rack over a few stones on the beach will pretty much do the same job.

THE RULES FOR SAFETY AND SUCCESS

Get ahead. Our recipes are designed to let you know what steps can be done in advance. Follow our THINK AHEAD instructions, so that when it's time to get grilling, you're all set.

Get organized. Be sure to have everything you need to hand. Outdoor grilling is high speed, high heat cooking. Once the food hits the flames, there's no time to run back to the kitchen for tongs, salt, or platter.

Let it be. Food will always stick to the grill rack initially, but once a crisp crust has formed, it can be turned or moved with ease. Don't poke, prod or attempt to turn food during the first minute of cooking.

Don't overcrowd the grill rack. An overloaded barbecue grill means food will steam, not sear. You don't want to miss out on the crisply caramelised crust that makes great grilled food what it is.

Check frequently for doneness. Use our suggested cooking times as a guideline. Start checking a few minutes before the food is due to be done. Once food is overcooked, it is tough and dry, and there's no turning the clock back.

Don't wander off. On the safety front, you are, after all, playing with fire, and accidents can happen. On the culinary front, food cooks quickly over hot coals and deserting your post can mean the difference between chargrilled and downright charred.

Clean up. A clean grill rack stops food from sticking. A grill rack encrusted with burnt food will result in coals that flare up and new food that tastes of old food. Brush the grill rack with a stiff wire brush while it is still hot, to loosen any charred remains.

The Tools

There are only a few accessories that we feel are really essential, with good-quality, long-handled tongs and a long metal spatula at the top of the list as must-haves for grilling.

1. Long-handled tongs
2. Long metal spatula
3. Hinged grill rack (round or square)
4. Flat metal skewers
5. Natural bristle basting brush
6. Bamboo skewers
7. Instant-read thermometer
8. Stiff wire brush for cleaning grill

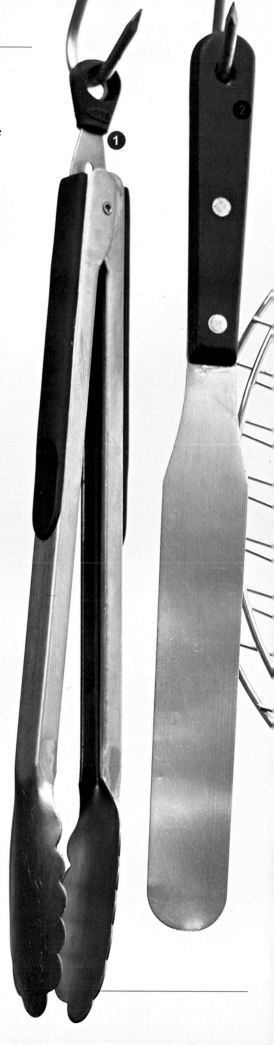

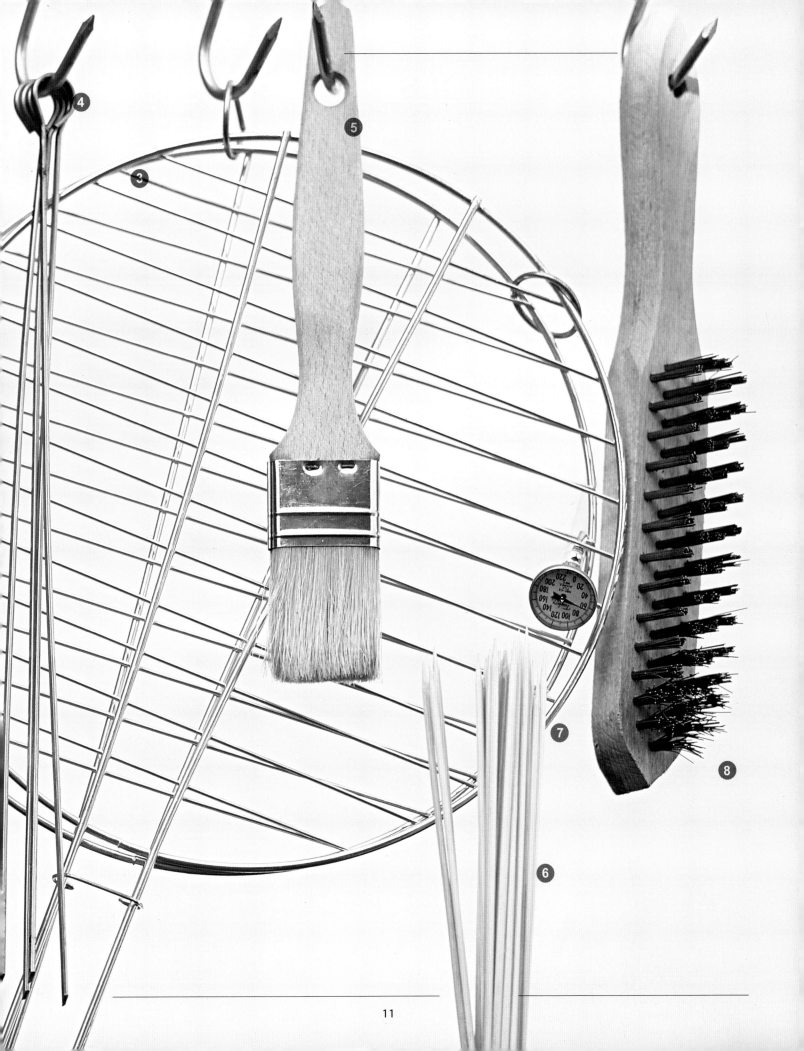

THE FIRE

Heat control is the key to successful grilling over charcoal. Building a good fire and judging its temperature are more crucial to success than the type or brand of barbecue grill you own or which type of fuel you use.

HOW TO BUILD IT

How much charcoal you use depends on how much and what kind of food you intend to grill. The more food you are cooking, the longer your fire needs to burn hot.

Bear in mind that it's easier to reduce heat than to raise it, so, as a general rule, start out with more charcoal than you think you'll need.

Spread the charcoal in an even layer about 5cm (2in) deep and 5cm (2in) wider on all sides than the total surface area of the food you are going to grill.

HOW HOT?

The appropriate time to test the temperature of a fire is when the flames have died down. The coals should be glowing red and covered with a light dusting of fine grey ash.

For an approximate guide, hold the palm of your hand flat about 12.5cm (5in) above the coals and count in seconds.

If you can only keep your hand there for:
- 1-2 seconds - the coals are hot
- 3-4 seconds - the coals are medium hot
- 5-6 seconds - the coals are medium
- 6-7 seconds - the coals are medium low
- 8-9 seconds - the coals are low

HOW TO CONTROL IT

If the fire burns too hot, reduce the heat by spreading out the coals.

If the fire burns too low, boost the heat by pushing the coals closer together and adding more charcoal to the outer edges of the fire.

For a two-level fire with hotter and cooler areas, spread some of the hot coals out in a single layer, to create an area of slightly lower heat to one side of the barbecue. Use the hand test (see above) to check the difference in heat intensity. You can then grill ingredients requiring different cooking temperatures simultaneously.

THE FOOD - DONENESS

Exact grilling times are difficult to predict. Fires burn differently under different conditions. Various factors out of your control, including wind and temperature, make outdoor cooking an empirical, rather than an exact, science.

Use our suggested cooking times as a guideline. Watch the clock and check food a few minutes before it is due to be done. Never wait until food is on the plate; always check at the grill.

Experienced chefs and seasoned grill-meisters rely on the touch test (see below) for dense meat like beef, lamb and pork. We think it is also important to double-check for doneness with a knife.

When grilling more delicate things like fish and chicken, use the methods illustrated below. For grilled chicken on the bone, because of the health issues, we urge a policy of seeing is believing.

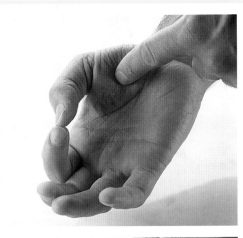

FORK TEST FOR FISH
Use a fork to prod the fish gently. It is done when the flesh is firm, just begining to flake and opaque through the centre but still moist.

TOUCH TEST FOR MEAT

The basic principle of the touch test is that meats become firmer as heat penetrates from the surface to the centre. Press the thickest part of the meat with your fingertip. The softer the meat is, the rarer it is. The firmer it is, the more well-done it is.

The touch test is a skill that can take some practice, but there is an easy shortcut for novice cooks. Press the meat with your finger. Compare the feel of the meat with the feel of the base of your thumb, as you move your thumb from fingertip to fingertip. The thumb muscle tenses and becomes progressively more resistant, corresponding to the different stages of doneness.

For rare, have your thumb touching your index finger (see above, top left).
For medium-rare, have your thumb touching your middle finger (see above, top right).
For medium, have your thumb touching your third finger (see above, bottom left).
For well-done, have your thumb touching your little finger (see above, bottom right).

KNIFE TEST FOR CHICKEN
Make a cut into the meat with a small, sharp knife. The flesh should be opaque throughout with no trace of pink at the bone.

THE KNOWLEDGE

THE PRINCIPLES

From a simple drizzle of olive oil to a complex blend of aromatic spices, there's a world of different flavours to transform grilled food into a bigger and bolder taste experience. There are two main ways of flavouring grilled food: before food is grilled and after food is removed from the fire.

• Flavouring before grilling generally calls for immersing food in a marinade or flavour mix. This immersion can be as brief as a quick dip or as lengthy as an overnight soak.

• Flavouring after grilling focuses on adding an extra flavour dimension to food hot off the grill. Sauces and salsas (pages 130-143) can be served as a flavourful complement to just-grilled foods. Spice mixes (pages 22-25) can be sprinkled or drizzled over food hot off the grill.

• Marinades and flavour mixes are composed of three key elements: acids, oils and flavourings. These elements perform three distinct functions: to tenderize, moisten and flavour.

ACIDS: TENDERIZE AND ADD FLAVOUR

Citrus juices, vinegars and yoghurt are all acid ingredients that will boost the intensity of any marinade with a bright, sharp tang. Here are a few general tips:

• Use freshly squeezed citrus juices for maximum zing.

• Choose your vinegar according to the level of acid bite you want in your marinade.

• Balsamic vinegar is the most versatile of vinegars. A combination of sweet and sharp, it is ideal for a marinade or to drizzle lightly over food hot from the fire.

• Yoghurt is a uniquely all-purpose acid for marinating in that it moistens as well as flavours and tenderizes.

OILS: PROVIDE MOISTURE

Lean, tender foods, such as fish and chicken, require the added moisture and protection provided by oil to combat the fierce heat of the fire. More resilient ingredients, such as beef and lamb, when marinated in acidic mixes, require oil to replace the moisture drawn out of the meat by the acid.

• Light, neutral oils, such as sunflower, contribute little flavour, but there are many other oils that have their own distinctive taste. Try using extra virgin olive oil or a nutty toasted sesame oil (see pages 20-21) for additional flavour.

• Oils can play their moisture-giving role at any stage of the grilling process: in marinades, as a baste during grilling, and as a flavour-packed mix to drizzle over grilled food just before serving.

ADDED FLAVOURS

Sweet flavourings take the sharp edge off an acidic marinade. Adding a bit of sugar to a flavour mix enhances the grilling process by helping to create a crispy caramelised crust on food exposed to the fire. Choose sweet flavourings that also add an extra dimension of flavour. We count fragrant honey, dark brown sugar and tangy pomegranate molasses (see pages 20 & 159) among our favourites.

Fresh flavourings add a fresh fragrance and depth to flavour mixes (see pages 20-21). Onions and garlic are pungent and vibrant. Asian flavours such as fresh ginger and lemon grass contribute a bright zing.

Fresh herbs should be chosen with care for the grill. Woody, robust herbs, such as oregano, rosemary and thyme, stand up to the strong flavour of food roasted over an open fire. Prolonged cooking over fierce heat eliminates the fragrant perfume of delicate herbs. Reserve them for making stuffings and for quickly grilled foods only.

Dried herbs are ideal flavour mixes for the grill (see pages 20-21). They contain aromatic oils that burst back into life when combined with the moisture of oil and the heat of the fire. Renew your supply of dried herbs regularly. On the grill, stale dried herbs will taste burnt and musty.

SALT AND PEPPER

Salt and pepper are extremely important flavourings for all grilled foods. Salt, however, draws out moisture, and with the moisture flavour, from uncooked food, so always add salt after grilling. For maximum flavour, pepper should be freshly ground or cracked (see page 19). A good pepper grinder is an essential item for all cooks who value real flavour.

• Our preference is always for sea salt, fine or flaked (see page 19).

• Soy sauce (both Chinese and Japanese), fish sauce and miso are the salts of Asia (see page 19). When using, you should not require additional salt.

CHILLIES
Don't be afraid of chillies - the capsicum family offers much more than just the addition of fiery heat. With so many different varieties available in so many different forms, barbecue cooks have a fabulous range of flavours at their fingertips.

• Look out for "pure" chilli powders ground from one variety of chilli (see page 18). No kitchen cupboard is complete without crushed chilli flakes, Tabasco and Thai sweet chilli sauce (see pages 19 & 158).

THE SPICE
SALT, PEPPER & CHILLIES

Discerning use of seasoning makes the difference between good and great food. Professional chefs constantly taste their food for levels of salt and heat. The quality of salt matters, as different salts have different flavours and different levels of saltiness. We prefer sea salt, fine or flaked.

Nothing compares with the flavour of freshly ground pepper. A pepper grinder is an essential kitchen tool for any cook. Chillies come in many varieties and forms. Whether fresh, dry or bottled, chillies will contribute flavour and aroma as well as peppery heat.

1 Crushed chilli flakes

2 Ancho chilli powder

3 Kashmiri chilli powder

4 Scotch bonnets

5 Fresh red and green chillies

6 Chipotle peppers in adobo

7 Chinese hot chilli sauce

8 Thai sweet chilli sauce

9 Tabasco sauce

10 Thai fish sauce

11 Soy sauce

12 Coarse sea salt

13 Fine sea salt

14 Peppercorns

15 Freshly ground pepper

THE SPICE ADDED FLAVOURS

Dedicated barbecue cooks should boast an international array of flavourings, condiments and sauces in their kitchen cupboard. Here are a few of our favourite flavourings from the global pantry.

1 Herbes de Provence
2 Greek oregano
3 Mexican oregano
4 Pomegranate molasses
5 Toasted sesame oil
6 Hoisin sauce
7 Rice wine vinegar
8 Citrus fruits
9 Red wine vinegar
10 Olive oil
11 Balsamic vinegar
12 Onions
13 Garlic
14 Smoked paprika
15 Hungarian paprika
16 Annatto
17 Tamarind
18 Miso
19 Wasabi
20 Fresh ginger

21 Pickled ginger
22 Lemon grass

CAROLINA HONEY GLAZE

MAKES 125ml (4floz)
2 tsp cajun seasoning
2 tbsp creamy dijon mustard
4 tbsp runny honey
2 tbsp cider vinegar or orange juice

Combine seasoning, mustard, honey and vinegar or juice. Use to marinate pork ribs up to 1 day in advance of grilling, pork chops up to 4 hours in advance, chicken wings up to 8 hours in advance and chicken breasts up to 4 hours in advance. Brush on more during grilling.

THINK AHEAD
Make up to 1 month in advance.
Cover and refrigerate.

CAJUN SEASONING

MAKES 125ml (4floz)
2 tbsp white peppercorns
2 tbsp black peppercorns
2 tbsp cayenne pepper
1 tbsp garlic powder
1 tbsp onion powder
2 tsp dried thyme
1 tsp dried mustard powder
½ tsp ground fennel

½ tsp dried oregano
¼ tsp ground cumin

Grind ingredients together (see page 161). Use 1 tbsp for 4 servings of meat. Rub steak up to 6 hours in advance of grilling, pork ribs up to 1 day in advance, prawns up to 2 hours in advance, fish up to 30 minutes in advance and chicken breasts up to 6 hours in advance.

THINK AHEAD
Make up to 3 months in advance. Store in an airtight container at room temperature.

CAJUN SEASONING

ACHIOTE SEASONING

CAROLINA HONEY GLAZE

ACHIOTE SEASONING

MAKES 125ml (4floz)

3 tbsp annatto seeds
2 tbsp dried oregano
2 tbsp cumin seeds
1 tbsp coriander seeds
1 tbsp black peppercorns
6 cloves
1 tbsp ground allspice
½ tbsp ground cinnamon

Grind the annatto seeds in a spice grinder until reduced to a powder. Toast oregano, cumin, coriander, peppercorns and cloves (see page 161). Leave to cool. Add toasted spices to crushed annatto and grind together to form a powder.
Use 2 tbsp per 4 servings of meat. Rub on to pork chops up to 4 hours in advance of grilling, prawns up to 2 hours in advance, fish up to 30 minutes in advance and chicken wings up to 8 hours in advance.

THINK AHEAD
Make up to 3 months in advance. Store in an airtight container at room temperature.

CHARMOULA

MAKES 150ml (5floz)

1 handful flat-leaf parsley
1 handful fresh coriander
4 garlic cloves, crushed
1 tsp paprika
1 tsp ground cumin
½ tsp ground coriander
¼ tsp cayenne pepper
2 tbsp lemon juice
2 tbsp olive oil

Place parsley, coriander, garlic, paprika, cumin, coriander, cayenne, lemon juice and oil in a food processor or blender; pulse to a paste. Use 1 recipe for 4 servings of meat. Use to marinate lamb up to 1 day in advance of grilling, prawns up to 2 hours in advance, fish up to 30 minutes in advance and chicken breasts up to 6 hours in advance.

THINK AHEAD
Make up to 3 days in advance. Cover and refrigerate.

RECADO ROJO

MAKES 125ml (4floz)

3 tbsp achiote seasoning
6 garlic cloves, crushed
3 tbsp orange or pineapple juice
2 tbsp red wine vinegar
1 tbsp olive oil
1 tbsp runny honey

Combine seasoning, garlic, juice, vinegar, oil and honey.
Use to marinate pork chops up to 8 hours in advance of grilling, chicken breasts up to 4 hours in advance, prawns up to 2 hours in advance and fish up to 30 minutes in advance.

THINK AHEAD
Make up to 1 day in advance. Cover and refrigerate.

CHARMOULA

RECADO ROJO

SPICY JERK RUB

MAKES 125ml (4floz)

6 spring onions, chopped
2 scotch bonnet chillies or
  3 jalapeños, seeded and chopped
2 tbsp grated fresh ginger
4 garlic cloves, crushed
1 medium onion, chopped
1 tsp ground allspice
1 tsp dried thyme
¼ tsp cinnamon
¼ tsp grated nutmeg
2 tsp salt
1 tsp black pepper
1 tbsp rum
1 tbsp cider vinegar
1 tbsp sunflower oil

Place spring onions, chillies, ginger, garlic, onion, allspice, thyme, cinnamon, nutmeg, salt, pepper, rum, vinegar and oil in a food processor or blender; pulse to a paste. Use 1 recipe per 4 servings. Rub on to meat just before grilling.

THINK AHEAD
Make up to 1 day in advance. Cover and refrigerate.

SPICY JERK RUB

JAMAICAN JERK SEASONING

MAKES 125ml (4floz)

2 tbsp onion powder
1 tbsp dried chives
1 tbsp dried thyme
1 tbsp ground allspice
1 tbsp salt
1 tbsp dark brown sugar
2 tsp black pepper
2 tsp cayenne pepper
2 tsp garlic powder
½ tsp grated nutmeg
½ tsp ground cinnamon

Combine onion powder, chives, thyme, allspice, salt, sugar, black pepper, cayenne pepper, garlic powder, nutmeg and cinnamon. Use 2 tbsp per 4 servings. Rub on to pork chops up to 4 hours in advance of grilling and chicken wings up to 8 hours in advance

THINK AHEAD
Make up to 3 months in advance. Store in an airtight container at room temperature.

GARAM MASALA

JAMAICAN JERK SEASONING

GARAM MASALA

MAKES 125ml (4floz)

3 tbsp cardamom pods
2½ tbsp cumin seeds
2 tbsp coriander seeds
1½ tbsp black peppercorns
1 tbsp cloves
2 tsp ground cinnamon
1 tsp grated nutmeg

Lightly crush cardamom pods. Discard skins and reserve seeds. Toast cardamom seeds, cumin, coriander, peppercorns and cloves (see page 161). Leave to cool. Crush toasted spices to a powder (see page 161). Blend with cinnamon and nutmeg. Use 2 tbsp per 4 servings. Rub on to pork chops up to 8 hours in advance of grilling, chicken breasts up to 4 hours in advance, prawns up to 2 hours in advance and fish up to 30 minutes in advance.

THINK AHEAD
Make up to 3 months in advance. Store in an airtight container at room temperature.

SPICY TANDOORI MIX

MAKES 3½ TBSP

2 tsp kashmiri or other red chilli powder
1 tbsp paprika
2 tbsp garam masala

Combine chilli powder, paprika and garam masala. Use 1 recipe per 4 servings. Rub on to lamb up to 1 day in advance of grilling, prawns up to 2 hours in advance, fish up to 30 minutes in advance and chicken breasts, wings and drumsticks up to 6 hours in advance.

JERKED HONEY RUM GLAZE

MAKES 125ml (4floz)

1 tsp jerk seasoning
4 tbsp runny honey
2 tsp dark rum

Combine seasoning, honey and rum. Brush on to meat just before and during grilling.

THINK AHEAD
Make up to 1 month in advance. Cover and refrigerate.

SPICY TANDOORI MIX

JERKED HONEY RUM GLAZE

MARINATING

Always cover food tightly while
marinating.

• The more completely the food is
coated with a marinade, the quicker
the flavouring process.
• If marinating in a dish, press cling
film directly on to the food in order
to expel any air.
• A sealed zip lock or oven roasting
plastic bag works very well to coat
and seal food completely in a
marinade.

Always use non-reactive containers
for marinating.

• Choose glass, pyrex, ceramic,
stainless steel and plastic.
• Never use aluminium, foil,
cast-iron or copper.

Never marinate foods beyond the
recommended time.
• The idea is to achieve taste
without toughness.
• If you over-marinate, what you
may gain in flavour, you'll sacrifice
in texture, as some acidic marinades
begin to break meat down if it is
left too long in a mix.

Always shake excess flavour mixes
off food before cooking.

• Oil that drips on to the coals
causes flare-ups, and flare-ups give
you burnt, not flame-kissed, food.

Never mix raw and cooked.

• Don't put grilled food back in the
same dish that you used for
marinating. Bacteria will still be in
the raw juices left behind in the
dish, so be sure to use a clean dish
for cooked food.

THE RECIPES

MEAT ON THE GRILL

BEEF ESSENTIALS

WHAT TO GRILL

Always choose beef that is liberally marbled with fat. We recommend buying steaks from the tenderloin, loin, sirloin or rump. Beef tastes best when cooked briefly and quickly over a high heat. This method yields succulent, juicy results.

GETTING IT READY

Well marbled beef needs only a light brush of oil before grilling. To prevent flare-ups, trim outer fat and shake off excess marinade before placing meat on the grill.

PUTTING IT ON

To achieve professional-looking, criss-cross markings on a steak, place it on the grill until grill markings are clearly visible across the underside of meat, about 1 minute. Rotate the steak through 60° (the angle between 12 and 2 o'clock) and leave to sear 1 minute more. Turn steak over and repeat on the opposite side.

TAKING IT OFF

Use your finger to touch test for doneness. The meat should feel soft, firm and juicy to the touch (see page 13).
When using a meat thermometer, beef should read for 65°C (150°F) for medium rare and 75°C (170°F) for well done.

RESTING

For juicy, tender beef, always allow meat to relax and juices to settle inside the meat before serving. Cover loosely with foil to keep warm and let stand for 5 minutes.

FINAL FLAVOURING

Salting beef before cooking draws out the flavourful juices and toughens the flesh. Always add seasoning at the last minute but be sure not to forget before serving.

CHARGRILLED SIRLOIN STEAK WITH GARLIC PARSLEY BUTTER

SERVES 4

4 - 250g (8oz) sirloin steaks, 2.5cm (1in) thick
1 tbsp melted butter
1 tsp black pepper
salt
4 - 1cm (½in) slices garlic parsley butter (see page 140)

Brush steaks with melted butter. Sprinkle with pepper. Grill according to instructions below. Sprinkle with salt and leave to rest for 5 minutes. Serve warm, topped with garlic parsley butter.

OUTDOOR
Grill over hot coals for 3 minutes per side for rare, 4 minutes per side for medium rare, 6 minutes per side for well done.

INDOOR
Preheat a ridged cast iron grill pan over high heat. Grill for 3 minutes per side for rare, 4 minutes per side for medium rare, 6 minutes per side for well done.

COOKS' NOTE
Any of the flavoured butters on pages 140-141 - blue cheese, black olive or coriander chilli - would be delicious melted over this succulent steak.

CHARGRILLED T-BONE STEAK WITH CHIMI CHURRI SAUCE

SERVES 4
2 - 750g (1½ lb) t-bone steaks, 2.5cm (1in) thick
1 tbsp olive oil
1 tsp black pepper
salt
1 recipe chimi churri sauce (see page 135)

Drizzle steaks with oil. Sprinkle with pepper. Grill according to instructions below. Sprinkle with salt. Leave to rest for 5 minutes. To serve, cut around the bone to release the meat. Cut the meat across into 5mm (¼in) slices. Serve hot with chimi churri sauce.

OUTDOOR
Grill over hot coals for 6 minutes per side for rare, 8 minutes per side for medium rare, 12 minutes per side for well done.

INDOOR
Preheat a ridged cast iron grill pan over high heat. Grill for 6 minutes per side for rare, 8 minutes per side for medium rare, 12 minutes per side for well done.

CHARGRILLED FILLET STEAK WITH SALSA VERDE

SERVES 4

4 - 175g (6oz) fillet steaks, 5cm (2in) thick
1 tbsp olive oil
1 tsp black pepper
salt
1 recipe salsa verde (see page 134)

ESSENTIAL EQUIPMENT
kitchen string

Tie a piece of string around the middle of each steak to ensure a neat shape and even cooking. Rub steaks with oil and pepper. Grill according to instructions below. Sprinkle with salt and leave to rest for 5 minutes. Cut string and remove. Serve warm, topped with salsa verde.

OUTDOOR
Grill over hot coals for 3 minutes per side for rare, 4 minutes per side for medium rare, 6 minutes per side for well done.

INDOOR
Preheat a ridged cast iron grill pan over high heat. Grill for 3 minutes per side for rare, 4 minutes per side for medium rare, 6 minutes per side for well done.

SESAME SOY SKEWERED STEAKS

SERVES 4

**8 - 60g (2oz) fillet steaks,
2.5cm (1in) thick**
4 spring onions

2 tbsp fresh grated ginger
3 garlic cloves, crushed
1 tsp crushed chilli flakes
½ tsp black pepper
1 tbsp sesame oil
2 tsp dark brown sugar
6 tbsp soy sauce
**1 tbsp rice vinegar or medium dry
sherry**
1 tbsp sesame seeds

ESSENTIAL EQUIPMENT
8 – 25cm (10in) presoaked bamboo skewers

Place 2 steaks side by side on a tray.
Push one skewer diagonally through
both steaks. Push a second skewer
diagonally, in the opposite direction to
the first skewer, to secure the 2 steaks
together, forming a cross with the 2
skewers. Thread the end of a spring
onion on to the pointed end of one
skewer. Thread the other end of the
spring onion on to the pointed end of the
second skewer. Repeat with remaining
steaks, skewers and spring onions.
Combine ginger, garlic, chilli flakes,
pepper, oil, sugar, soy sauce, vinegar or
sherry and sesame seeds in a bowl. Pour
mixture over skewered steaks. Cover
and refrigerate for 30 minutes. Grill
according to instructions below.
Serve hot.

OUTDOOR
Grill over medium-hot
coals for 3 minutes per
side for rare, 4 minutes
per side for medium-rare,
6 minutes per side for
well done.

INDOOR
Preheat overhead grill.
Grill for 3 minutes per
side for rare, 4 minutes
per side for medium-rare,
6 minutes per side for
well done.

THINK AHEAD
Skewer and marinate steaks up to 8 hours in advance.
Cover and refrigerate.

SPICED BEEF FAJITAS WITH SALSA FRESCA AND GUACAMOLE

SERVES 4

FOR MARINADE

2 garlic cloves, crushed
½ tsp crushed chilli flakes
½ tsp ground cumin
½ tsp dried oregano
¼ tsp ground allspice
2 tbsp mexican beer, or lager
1 tbsp olive oil

500g (1lb) rump steak, cut 2.5cm (1in) thick

FOR GUACAMOLE

2 fresh green chillies, seeded and finely chopped
2 tbsp finely chopped fresh coriander
4 tbsp lime juice
2 medium avocados, chopped
salt, black pepper

4 flour tortillas
salt, black pepper
1 handful shredded lettuce
1 recipe salsa fresca (see page 133)
125ml (4floz) sour cream

OUTDOOR
Grill over hot coals for 5 minutes per side for rare, 7 minutes per side for medium rare, 10 minutes per side for well done. Warm tortillas by setting directly over grill for 30 seconds each side.

INDOOR
Preheat a ridged cast iron grill pan over high heat. Grill for 5 minutes per side for rare, 7 minutes per side for medium rare, 10 minutes per side for well done. Warm tortillas by placing in grill pan for 30 seconds each side.

THINK AHEAD
Marinate beef up to 1 day in advance. Cover and refrigerate. Make guacamole up to 1 day in advance. Cover tightly with cling film, pressing directly on the guacamole to prevent contact with air, and refrigerate.

COOKS' NOTE
Fajitas are a classic of Tex-Mex cuisine. Skirt steak is the traditional cut to use. It is well worth asking your butcher for this lean, flat, intensely flavourful steak. Grill as directed for a truly authentic Tex-Mex fajita.

For marinade, combine garlic, chilli flakes, cumin, oregano, allspice, beer and oil. Add steak and turn to coat. Cover and refrigerate for 1 hour. For guacamole, combine chillies, coriander, lime juice and avocado. Mash with a potato masher until well combined but still chunky. Add salt and pepper to taste. Cover and refrigerate. Grill steak according to instructions opposite. Leave to stand for 5 minutes before carving on the diagonal into 1cm (½in) thick slices. Warm tortillas according to instructions opposite. Place steak slices on warmed tortillas. Sprinkle with salt and pepper. Top with lettuce, salsa fresca, guacamole and sour cream. Roll up and serve hot.

HUNGARIAN SPICED BEEF SKEWERS WITH SOUR CREAM

SERVES 4

500g (1lb) minced chuck steak
1 onion, grated
4 garlic cloves, crushed
2 tsp paprika
1 tsp dried marjoram
1 tsp ground caraway
1 tsp black pepper
2 tsp salt
salt and black pepper to sprinkle
150ml (5floz) sour cream to serve
1 recipe chargrilled garlic potato slices (see page 120), optional

ESSENTIAL EQUIPMENT
8 – 25cm (10in) presoaked bamboo skewers

Place minced steak, onion, garlic, paprika, marjoram, caraway, pepper and salt in a food processor; pulse until combined. Divide into 8 equal-sized portions. With wet hands, mould each portion round a separate skewer, shaping it into a sausage, about 20cm (8in) long. Grill according to instructions below. Sprinkle with salt and pepper. Serve hot with sour cream and chargrilled garlic potato slices, optional.

OUTDOOR
Grill over medium-hot coals, turning every 2 minutes, until well browned but still juicy and slightly pink inside, 8-10 minutes.

INDOOR
Preheat overhead grill. Grill, turning every 2 minutes, until well browned but still juicy and slightly pink inside, 8-10 minutes.

THINK AHEAD
Prepare and skewer satays up to 1 day in advance. Cover with cling film and refrigerate.

COOKS' NOTE
If you can find it, use Hungarian paprika, which is superior to the more widely available Spanish paprika. It has a sweet, sun-dried flavour and a bright colour.

CORIANDER BEEF SATAYS WITH HONEY TAMARIND GLAZE

SERVES 4

500g (1lb) minced chuck
   steak
2 tbsp grated fresh ginger
2 garlic cloves, crushed
1 onion, grated
1 handful fresh coriander
   leaves

1 tsp ground coriander
1 tsp ground turmeric
1 tsp chilli powder
½ tsp ground cumin
½ tsp ground cardamom
2 tsp salt
½ tsp black pepper

FOR GLAZE

1 tbsp grated fresh ginger
1 garlic clove, crushed
1½ tbsp tamarind paste
1½ tbsp runny honey

salt, black pepper

ESSENTIAL EQUIPMENT
8 – 35cm (14in) flat metal skewers

Place minced steak, ginger, garlic, onion, fresh coriander, ground coriander, turmeric, chilli powder, cumin, cardamom, salt and pepper in a food processor; pulse until combined. Divide into 8 equal-sized portions. With wet hands, mould each portion round a separate skewer, shaping it into a sausage, about 20cm (8in) long.

For glaze, combine ginger, garlic, tamarind and honey. Grill according to instructions below. Sprinkle with salt and pepper. Serve hot.

OUTDOOR
Grill over medium-hot coals, brushing with glaze, turning every 2 minutes, until well browned but still juicy and slightly pink inside, 8-10 minutes.

INDOOR
Preheat overhead grill. Brush with glaze and grill, turning every 2 minutes, until well browned but still juicy and slightly pink inside, 8-10 minutes.

THINK AHEAD
Prepare and skewer satays up to 1 day in advance. Cover with cling film and refrigerate.

COOKS' NOTE
Dark, shiny tamarind paste - sometimes referred to as concentrate - has a refreshing, sharp citrus flavour. It is usually available from Asian and Middle-Eastern stores. If you can't find it, use tamarind pulp. For this recipe, dissolve 1 tbsp pulp in 1 tbsp boiling water, then cool and sieve before using.

BEST BURGER WITH BLUE CHEESE BUTTER

SERVES 4

500g (1lb) minced chuck steak
2 tsp salt
1 tsp black pepper

4 - 1cm (½ in) slices blue cheese
butter (see page 140)
4 sesame hamburger rolls, halved

Combine minced steak with salt and pepper. Divide into 4 equal-sized pieces and gently shape into 4 burgers about 2.5cm (1in) thick. Grill burgers and warm rolls according to instructions below. Top with butter and serve hot in sesame rolls.

OUTDOOR
Grill over hot coals for 3 minutes per side for rare, 4 minutes per side for medium rare, 5 minutes per side for well done. Place rolls cut side down on grill until warm and lightly golden, 1 minute.

INDOOR
Preheat a ridged cast iron grill pan over high heat. Grill for 3 minutes per side for rare, 4 minutes per side for medium rare, 5 minutes per side for well done. Place rolls cut side down on grill pan until warm and lightly golden, 1 minute.

THINK AHEAD
Shape burgers up to 1 day in advance. Cover with cling film and refrigerate.

COOKS' NOTE
Over-handling the meat when shaping will result in a tough, dry burger. To guarantee a juicy burger, handle the meat as little as possible.

BEST BURGER VARIATIONS
HERBED BURGER
Add 2 tsp fresh thyme leaves or 1 tsp dried thyme, 1 crushed garlic clove and 1 tbsp finely chopped onion to the minced steak. Serve with garlic parsley butter (see page 140) in place of blue cheese butter.

SPICY BURGER
Add ½ tsp tabasco, 1 tbsp worcester-shire sauce and 1 tsp creamy dijon mustard to the minced steak. Serve with coriander chilli butter (see page 140) in place of blue cheese butter.

PORK ESSENTIALS

WHAT TO GRILL

Small, lean and tender cuts, such as chops and ribs, will stay moist during cooking if they are marinated before and basted well during grilling. Larger cuts need to be cut into strips or cubes, and skewered. It is important for pork to be completely cooked through. Sausages are ideal for the grill, as there is plenty of evenly distributed fat to keep the meat moist throughout the cooking time.

GETTING IT READY

Trim off excess fat to avoid flare-ups. Unlike lamb and beef, the fat surrounds pork meat rather than marbling it, so to achieve meat which is cooked through but still juicy, pork should be marinated or brushed with oil before going on the grill.

TAKING IT OFF

Pork should be cooked until the internal temperature reaches 65°C (150°F). The meat should be opaque throughout but still moist.

RESTING

For juicy, tender pork, always allow meat to relax and juices to settle inside the meat before serving. Cover loosely with foil to keep warm, and let stand for 5 minutes.

FINAL FLAVOURING

Salting pork before cooking draws out the flavourful juices and toughens the flesh. Always add seasoning at the last minute, but be sure not to forget.

MEXICAN SPICED PORK CHOPS WITH PINEAPPLE LIME SALSA

SERVES 4

4 pork chops, 2.5cm (1in) thick
4 garlic cloves, crushed
1 tsp dried oregano
1 tsp ground cumin
½ tsp ground coriander
½ tsp black pepper
¼ tsp ground cinnamon

2 tbsp red wine vinegar
3 tbsp orange juice
1 tbsp runny honey
1 tbsp olive oil
salt, black pepper
1 recipe pineapple lime salsa
  (see page 134)

Trim off excess fat from the chops. With scissors, cut snips through the remaining fat at 4cm (1½in) intervals. Combine garlic, oregano, cumin, coriander, black pepper, cinnamon, vinegar, orange juice, honey and oil. Pour mixture over chops, turning several times to coat thoroughly. Cover and refrigerate for 4 hours. Grill according to instructions below. Sprinkle with salt and pepper. Serve hot with pineapple lime salsa.

OUTDOOR
Grill over medium-hot coals until there is no trace of pink near the bone but the pork is still juicy, 8-10 minutes per side.

INDOOR
Preheat a ridged cast iron grill pan over high heat. Grill until there is no trace of pink near the bone but the pork is still juicy, 8–10 minutes per side.

THINK AHEAD
Marinate pork up to 1 day in advance. Cover and refrigerate.

ROSEMARY PEPPERED PORK CHOPS

SERVES 4

4 pork chops, 2.5cm (1in) thick
4 garlic cloves
2 tbsp whole black peppercorns
3 tbsp fresh rosemary leaves
  or 1 tbsp dried rosemary
1 tsp fennel seeds
¼ tsp crushed chilli flakes
1 tbsp lemon juice
3 tbsp olive oil
lemon wedges

Trim off excess fat from the chop. With scissors, cut snips through the remaining fat at 4cm (1½in) intervals. Place garlic, peppercorns, rosemary, fennel seeds, chilli flakes, lemon juice and oil in a food processor or blender; pulse to a coarse paste. Rub the paste over both sides of the chops. Grill according to instructions below. Sprinkle with salt. Serve hot with lemon wedges.

OUTDOOR
Grill over medium-hot coals until there is no trace of pink near the bone but the pork is still juicy, 8-10 minutes per side.

INDOOR
Preheat a ridged cast iron grill pan over high heat. Grill until there is no trace of pink near the bone but the pork is still juicy, 8-10 minutes per side.

THINK AHEAD
Rub pork with paste up to 2 hours in advance. Cover and refrigerate.

COOKS' NOTE
Snipping the outer fat with scissors prevents the chops from curling and shrinking during cooking, allowing them to remain flat and to cook evenly.

BALSAMIC PEPPERED PORK CHOPS

SERVES 4

4 pork chops, 2.5cm (1in) thick
4 garlic cloves
2 tbsp whole black peppercorns
1 tbsp dried thyme
¼ tsp crushed chilli flakes
1 tbsp balsamic vinegar
3 tbsp olive oil
extra balsamic for basting

Trim off excess fat from the chop. With scissors, cut snips through the remaining fat at 4cm (1½in) intervals. Place garlic, peppercorns, thyme, chilli flakes, vinegar and oil in a food processor or blender; pulse to a coarse paste. Rub the paste over both sides of the chops. Grill according to instructions below. Serve hot.

OUTDOOR
Grill over medium-hot coals, basting with the extra balsamic vinegar, until there is no trace of pink near the bone but the pork is still juicy, 8-10 minutes per side.

INDOOR
Preheat a ridged cast iron grill pan over high heat. Grill, basting with the extra balsamic vinegar, until there is no trace of pink near the bone but the pork is still juicy, 8-10 minutes per side.

THINK AHEAD
Rub pork with paste up to 2 hours in advance. Cover and refrigerate.

COOKS' NOTE
Snipping the outer fat with scissors prevents the chops from curling and shrinking during cooking, allowing them to remain flat and to cook evenly.

SLICING AND SKEWERING PORK FILLET
Slice the pork fillet against the grain of the meat into strips 0.5cm (¼in) thick and about 10-15cm (4-6in) long.

Lay the strips flat on a board, side by side. Thread on to 3 parallel skewers.

SWEET SOY GLAZED PORK

SERVES 4

500g (1lb) pork fillet, sliced and skewered (see opposite)	4 tbsp hoisin sauce
6 tbsp soy sauce	3 tbsp medium dry sherry
3 tbsp tomato ketchup	3 tbsp runny honey
	3 tbsp dark brown sugar

ESSENTIAL EQUIPMENT
3 – 35cm (14in) flat metal skewers

Combine soy sauce, ketchup, hoisin, sherry, honey and sugar. Set aside 6 tbsp of the mixture. Spread remaining mixture over both sides of the pork skewers. Grill according to instructions below. Serve hot with the remaining mixture drizzled over.

OUTDOOR
Grill over medium-hot coals until pork is opaque but still juicy, 3 minutes per side.

INDOOR
Preheat overhead grill. Grill until pork is opaque but still juicy, 3 minutes per side.

THINK AHEAD
Marinate pork up to 4 hours in advance. Cover and refrigerate.

SWEET SOY GLAZED PORK

SPICY PORK SATAY

SERVES 4

500g (1lb) pork fillet,
sliced and skewered
 (see page 46)
2 lemon grass stalks
1 tbsp grated fresh ginger
2 garlic cloves, crushed
1 onion
2 tsp ground fennel

2 tsp ground cumin
2 tsp ground coriander
1 tsp turmeric
1 tbsp lime juice
1 tbsp sunflower oil
salt, black pepper
1 recipe spicy peanut sauce
 (see page 136) to serve

ESSENTIAL EQUIPMENT
12 – 25cm (10in) presoaked bamboo skewers

OUTDOOR
Grill over medium-hot coals until pork is opaque but still juicy, 3 minutes per side.

INDOOR
Preheat overhead grill. Grill until pork is opaque but still juicy, 3 minutes per side.

THINK AHEAD
Marinate pork up to 1 day in advance. Cover and refrigerate.

COOKS' NOTE
For maximum flavour, be sure to toast and crush all the spices freshly (see page 161).

Remove and discard the tough outer skin from the lemon grass stalks and roughly chop. Place lemon grass, ginger, garlic, onion, fennel, cumin, coriander, turmeric, lime juice and oil in a food processor or blender; pulse to form a smooth paste. Spread paste over both sides of the pork skewers. Cover and refrigerate for 4 hours. Grill according to instructions opposite. Sprinkle with salt and pepper. Serve hot with spicy peanut sauce.

THAI SWEET & SOUR RIBS

SERVES 4

2kg (4lb) pork spareribs
1 red onion, finely chopped
2 garlic cloves, crushed
1 tbsp grated fresh ginger
1 tbsp sunflower oil
125ml (4floz) pineapple juice
2 tbsp fish sauce
4 tbsp tomato purée
4 tbsp lime juice
2 tbsp runny honey
6 tbsp thai sweet chilli sauce

Separate ribs by slicing between the bones with a large knife or cleaver. Simmer separated ribs in a large pan of salted water until just tender, about 30 minutes. Drain. Rinse under cold running water and drain again. Leave to cool completely. Place onion, garlic, ginger and oil in a small pan. Stir fry over medium heat until softened, 5-10 minutes. Add pineapple juice, fish sauce, tomato purée, lime juice, honey and 2 tbsp sweet chilli sauce. Bring to the boil. Simmer gently until thick, 10 minutes. Leave to cool completely. Brush the sweet sour mixture over the ribs. Grill according to instructions below, basting with the remaining chilli sauce throughout. Serve hot.

OUTDOOR
Grill over medium-hot coals, turning frequently and basting, until brown and crusty, 15 minutes.

INDOOR
Preheat overhead grill. Grill, removing from under the grill every 5 minutes to baste, until brown and crusty, 15 minutes.

THINK AHEAD
Pre-cook the ribs up to 1 day in advance. Cool completely. Cover with cling film and refrigerate. Make glaze up to 1 day in advance. Cover and refrigerate.

COOKS' NOTE
Pre-cook the ribs in simmering water to remove the layer of outer fat. This not only prevents flare-ups during cooking, but allows the rib meat to stay tender and juicy inside and crispy on the outside.

RIB VARIATION
SPICED HOISIN RIBS

Omit all ingredients for the sweet sour mixture. Combine instead 8 tbsp hoisin sauce, ½ tsp chinese five-spice, 4 crushed garlic cloves, 2 tbsp grated fresh ginger, 2 tbsp medium dry sherry, 4 tbsp soy sauce, 2 tbsp hot chinese sauce and 8 tbsp dark brown sugar. Reserve 2 tbsp hoisin mixture for basting. Brush remaining mixture over ribs. Grill according to recipe above.

GARLIC MUSTARD PORK SKEWERS

SERVES 4

2 garlic cloves, crushed
2 tbsp worcestershire sauce
2 tbsp soy sauce
4 tbsp tomato ketchup
1 tbsp tomato purée
1 tsp tabasco
2 tbsp cider vinegar
2 tsp paprika

2 tbsp grainy dijon mustard
2 tbsp creamy dijon mustard
4 tbsp runny honey
500g (1lb) pork fillet, sliced and skewered (see page 46)

ESSENTIAL EQUIPMENT
3 – 35cm (14in) flat metal skewers

Combine garlic, worcestershire sauce, soy sauce, tomato ketchup, tomato purée, tabasco, vinegar, paprika, mustards and honey. Set aside 6 tbsp of the glaze. Spread remaining glaze over both sides of the pork skewers. Grill according to instructions below. Serve hot with the remaining glaze.

OUTDOOR
Grill over medium-hot coals until pork is opaque but still juicy, 3 minutes per side.

INDOOR
Preheat overhead grill. Grill until pork is opaque but still juicy, 3 minutes per side.

THINK AHEAD
Marinate pork up to 4 hours in advance. Cover and refrigerate.

COOKS' NOTE
If you can find it, use smoked paprika for this recipe. Smoked paprika is a speciality paprika from Spain. Unlike other paprikas, the peppers are not sun-dried, but oak-smoked, before being ground. This gives it a deep, rusty red colour and a distinctive smoky flavour. Smoked paprika is available from mail order and speciality stores (see page 167).

MAKING SAUSAGES

Run water through the casings to check for any holes or tears.

Gather casing up on to the nozzle until you reach the end of the casing.

Twist the top of the bag until the filling is visible in the nozzle, to clear any air pockets before you begin.

Gently squeeze the bag so that the casing fills evenly and forms a long sausage.

Prick all over with a toothpick to prevent the sausage from bursting during cooking.

COOKS' NOTE
Most butchers will sell you sausage casing if you give them some advance notice. The casing should come packed in salt.

TOULOUSE SAUSAGES

SERVES 4
500g (1lb) piece boneless streaky pork belly
2 tsp salt
1 tsp black pepper
100ml (3½ floz) cold water
1 metre (3ft) sausage casings

ESSENTIAL EQUIPMENT
Piping bag fitted with large plain nozzle, hinged grill rack or 2 flat metal skewers

Remove the rind from the pork and cut into 2.5cm (1in) cubes. Place pork cubes, salt, pepper and water in a food processor; pulse until the ground pork begins to form a ball.

Rinse the casings under cold running water and soak in a large bowl of cold water. This will remove excess salt and make the casings more pliable. Run water through casings to check for any holes or tears. Insert the nozzle into one end of the casing. Gather casing up on to the nozzle until you reach the other end of the casing. Fill the piping bag with sausagemeat. Twist the top of the bag until the filling is visible in the nozzle. Gently squeeze the top of the piping bag so that the casing fills evenly with the sausagemeat and forms a long sausage. Prick the finished sausage all over with a toothpick. See illustrations opposite for guidance.

For outdoor grilling, place the coiled sausage in a hinged grill rack, if using. Alternatively, and for indoor cooking, secure by pushing 2 skewers across each other through the coiled sausage. Grill according to instructions below. Serve hot.

OUTDOOR
Grill over medium-hot coals until browned and cooked through, 8-10 minutes per side.

INDOOR
Preheat overhead grill. Grill until browned and cooked through, 8-10 minutes per side.

THINK AHEAD
Make sausages up to 1 day in advance. Cover with cling film and refrigerate.

SAUSAGE VARIATIONS
GARLIC SAUSAGES

Add 60g (2oz) crushed garlic cloves to the food processor with the pork cubes, salt, pepper and water. Prepare and stuff casing according to recipe above.

SPICY SAUSAGES

Add 2 tsp paprika, 1 seeded and finely chopped fresh red chilli and 4 crushed garlic cloves in the food processor with the pork cubes, salt, pepper and water. Prepare and stuff casing according to recipe above.

LAMB ESSENTIALS

PERFECT MEAT FOR THE GRILL
Lamb is the original inspiration for the Mediterranean's great tradition of outdoor feasting. The meat is liberally and evenly marbled with fat, making it the ideal meat for the grill.

GETTING IT READY
Cut off excess fat to avoid flare-ups. Pull off the thin transparent membrane surrounding the meat and trim off any connective tissue.

PUTTING IT ON
Remove small cuts from the refrigerator 30 minutes, and large cuts 45 minutes, before grilling. To avoid flare-ups, shake off excess marinade before placing on the grill.

TAKING IT OFF
The surface of lamb cooks much faster than the interior, which results in a crisp, browned exterior with juicy meat inside. Use your finger to touch test for doneness. The meat should feel soft, firm and juicy to the touch (see page 13). When using a meat thermometer, lamb should read 65°C (150°F) for rare, and 75°C (170°F) for well done.

RESTING
For juicy, tender lamb, and in particular for large cuts, allow meat to relax and the juices to settle inside the meat before carving. Cover loosely with foil to keep warm and let stand for 10 minutes.

FINAL FLAVOURING
Salting lamb before cooking draws out the flavourful juices and toughens the flesh. Always add seasoning at the last minute, but be sure not to forget before serving.

BONING AND HERB-SKEWERING CHOPS

Trim off excess fat from cutlets. Cut around the bone to release the meat.

Pull the flap round each chop to make a round shape. With a small, sharp knife make a slit through the chop, passing first through the flap. Push the sharp end of the rosemary sprig through the slit to secure.

THINK AHEAD
Bone and skewer chops up to 1 day in advance. Cover and refrigerate.

COOKS' NOTE
You can use a bamboo or metal skewer instead of a rosemary sprig.

ROSEMARY LAMB CHOPS WITH MUSTARD MINT DRESSING

SERVES 4

8 - 10cm (4in) rosemary sprigs
8 lamb loin chops, boned
  (see opposite)
1 garlic clove, crushed
2 tsp black pepper
1 tbsp balsamic vinegar
1 tbsp olive oil
salt

FOR DRESSING
1 tbsp creamy dijon mustard
2 tbsp finely chopped fresh mint
3 tbsp lemon juice
6 tbsp olive oil
salt, black pepper

For skewers, strip the leaves from the rosemary stalks, leaving a few leaves at one end of each stalk. Sharpen the other end to a point with a knife. Use sprigs to skewer lamb (see opposite). Combine garlic, pepper, vinegar and oil. Rub on to both sides of lamb. Cover and refrigerate for 30 minutes.

For dressing, combine mustard, mint and lemon juice. Gradually whisk in oil to make a thick dressing. Add salt and pepper to taste. Grill skewered lamb according to instructions below. Sprinkle with salt and pepper. Spoon over dressing and serve hot.

OUTDOOR
Grill over hot coals for 3 minutes per side for medium rare, 5 minutes per side for well done.

INDOOR
Preheat a ridged cast iron grill pan over high heat. Grill for 3 minutes per side for medium rare, 5 minutes per side for well done.

THINK AHEAD
Skewer and rub lamb up to 1 day in advance. Cover tightly with cling film and refrigerate. Make dressing up to 4 hours in advance. Cover and store at room temperature.

BUTTERFLIED LEG OF LAMB WITH ANCHOVY, PROSCIUTTO AND PARSLEY

SERVES 4 - 6

FOR PASTE
60g (2oz) prosciutto
6 anchovy fillets
1 handful flat-leaf parsley
2 garlic cloves
1 tbsp balsamic vinegar

ESSENTIAL EQUIPMENT
2 - 35cm (14in) flat metal skewers

2kg (4lb) leg of lamb, butterflied
(see opposite)
2 tbsp balsamic vinegar for drizzling
salt, black pepper
1 recipe salsa verde (see page 134)

Place prosciutto, anchovies, parsley, garlic and vinegar in a food processor or blender; pulse to a smooth paste. Place lamb skin side down. With a sharp knife, cut 1cm (½in) deep slits across the lamb about 5cm (2in) apart. Push the paste deep into the slits. Insert skewers diagonally from opposite corners through butterflied lamb. Grill according to instructions below, drizzling balsamic vinegar on both sides during cooking. Remove to a board, cover with foil and leave to rest for 10 minutes before slicing. Sprinkle with salt and pepper. Serve warm with salsa verde, optional.

OUTDOOR
Grill over medium-hot coals, turning once, for 15 minutes per side for medium rare or 20 minutes per side for well done.

INDOOR
Preheat overhead grill. Arrange lamb on a wire rack over an oven tray. Grill, turning once, for 15 minutes per side for medium rare or 20 minutes per side for well done.

THINK AHEAD
Make paste up to 2 days in advance. Cover and refrigerate. Prepare lamb and stuff with paste up to 1 day in advance. Double wrap in cling film and refrigerate. Remove from refrigerator 45 minutes before grilling.

COOKS' NOTE
Skewering the butterflied lamb helps keep the meat together and also makes it easier to move on the grill.

BUTTERFLYING LEG OF LAMB
Put the leg of lamb on a board, skin side down. Cut round the exposed bone at the wide end of the leg. Cut the bone free at the joint and detach. Cut a slit along the length of the bone to expose and loosen. Use short, shallow cuts and scrape with the knife blade to release the meat from the bone. Remove bone.
Keeping the blade of the knife horizontal, make a lengthwise slit along the thick section of the meat next to the cavity left by the leg bone. Open out the flap and spread the meat flat like a book. Make another horizontal cut into the thick meat opposite and open out flat to form a "butterfly" shape with the entire piece.

COOKS' NOTE
Butterflying is a very useful technique for preparing meat for the grill. It allows the home chef to grill a large cut of meat in a quarter of time it would take to roast it. You'll find a boned joint easier to carve with less waste.

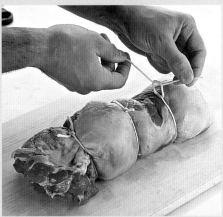

ROLLING BUTTERFLIED LEG OF LAMB
Spread the meat evenly with seasoning and herbs. Roll up lengthwise as tightly as possible. Place roll seam side down on a board.

Secure the roll with string. Starting in the centre, tie the meat tightly at 2cm (¾in) intervals.

Cut between the strings to make equal-sized steaks.

COOKS' NOTE
This technique transforms a leg of lamb into boneless individual portions that have all the flavour of the whole cut, but can be cooked and served with speed and ease.

LEG OF LAMB STEAKS WITH BLACK OLIVE BUTTER

SERVES 4

2kg (4lb) leg of lamb, butterflied (see page 54)
1 tbsp salt
2 tsp black pepper

3 tbsp stripped fresh thyme leaves
1 recipe black olive butter (see page 140)

ESSENTIAL EQUIPMENT
kitchen string

Sprinkle the meat evenly with salt, pepper and thyme. Roll up, secure with string and cut into steaks (see opposite). Grill according to instructions below. Just before removing from the grill, top each steak with a slice of black olive butter.

OUTDOOR
Grill over medium hot coals, turning once, 5 minutes per side for medium rare or 8 minutes per side for well done.

INDOOR
Preheat a ridged cast iron grill over high heat. Grill, turning once, 5 minutes per side for medium rare or 8 minutes per side for well done.

THINK AHEAD
Roll, stuff and slice lamb up to 2 days in advance. Double wrap in cling film and refrigerate. Remove to room temperature 20 minutes before grilling.

COOKS' NOTE
For a butter-free alternative, we suggest serving the lamb steaks with spiced chickpea sauce (see page 137) in place of the black olive butter.

BUTTERFLIED LEG OF LAMB PERSILLADE

2kg (4lb) leg of lamb, butterflied (see page 54)
1 tbsp salt
2 tsp black pepper
6 garlic cloves, sliced
2 handfuls flat-leaf parsley, roughly chopped

ESSENTIAL EQUIPMENT
3 - 35cm (14in) flat metal skewers

Prepare the butterflied lamb for stuffing by slicing it open again (see opposite). Sprinkle the meat evenly with salt and pepper. Spread garlic and parsley over one half of the meat (see opposite). Fold in half and secure with skewers (see opposite). Grill according to instructions below. Remove to a cutting board, cover with foil and leave to rest for 5 minutes before slicing.

OUTDOOR
Grill over medium hot coals, turning once, for 15 minutes per side for medium rare or 20 minutes per side for well done.

INDOOR
Preheat overhead grill. Arrange lamb on a wire rack over an oven tray. Grill, turning once, for 15 minutes per side for medium rare or 20 minutes per side for well done.

THINK AHEAD
Slice, stuff and skewer lamb up to 2 days in advance. Double wrap in cling film and refrigerate. Remove to room temperature 45 minutes before grilling.

COOKS' NOTE
Serve with potato focaccia with thyme (see page 155) or creamy potato salad with celery and chives (see page 148).

STUFFING BUTTERFLIED LEG OF LAMB
Hold the meat firmly with the flat of your hand. Keeping the blade of the knife horizontal, slice into the thickest part of the meat again to open an additional flap for stuffing.

Sprinkle over the stuffing.

Thread the skewers through both sides of the meat to secure.

COOKS' NOTE
Here we slice a butterflied leg in half again to make a pocket for flavourful stuffing. This makes spectacular presentation that never fails to impress.

BONING SHOULDER
Place shoulder skin side down. Cut a slit along the length of the two bones to expose. Cut and scrape the meat free from the shoulder bone. Cut through the joint to free the shoulder bone.

Cut through the meat on either side of the blade bone. Scraping the bone free, pull away the blade bone from the meat.

CUBING BONELESS SHOULDER
Trim off excess fat. Cut the meat into 4cm (1½in) strips.
Cut the strips into 4cm (1½in) cubes. You will need 20 cubes for 4 servings.

THINK AHEAD
Bone and cube lamb shoulder up to 2 days in advance. Cover tightly with cling film and refrigerate.

COOKS' NOTE
You need about 1kg (2lb) lamb shoulder on the bone to yield about 500g (1lb) boneless lamb. If you prefer a leaner cut, choose boneless leg of lamb.

CORIANDER LAMB PITTA WRAP

SERVES 4

500g (1lb) boneless lamb, cut into 4cm (1½in) cubes (see opposite)

½ medium onion
2 garlic cloves

FOR MARINADE
1½ tsp ground coriander
½ tsp ground cumin
¼ tsp ground allspice
¼ tsp ground cinnamon
2 tbsp lemon juice
2 tbsp olive oil
1 tomato, halved

FOR WRAP
4 pitta or flatbreads
1 handful shredded lettuce
4 tomatoes, cut into wedges
16 fresh mint leaves
1 recipe lemon tahini sauce (see page 132)
salt, black pepper

ESSENTIAL EQUIPMENT
4 – 35cm (14in) flat metal skewers

Place coriander, cumin, allspice, cinnamon, lemon juice, oil, tomato, onion and garlic in food processor or blender; pulse to form a thick paste. In a bowl, combine paste with lamb cubes, tossing to coat evenly. Cover and refrigerate for 2 hours. Thread lamb on to skewers. Grill according to instructions below. Split open and separate each pitta into 2 halves. Stack 2 pitta halves cut side up. Using a fork, slide the lamb pieces from 1 skewer on to the pitta. Top with a quarter of the lettuce, tomatoes and mint. Spoon over lemon tahini sauce. Sprinkle with salt and pepper and roll up. Repeat with remaining pitta, lamb, lettuce, tomatoes, mint and tahini sauce. Serve hot.

OUTDOOR
Grill over medium-hot coals, turning every 2 minutes, until well browned but still juicy and slightly pink inside, 8-10 minutes. Place pitta halves directly on the grill until just warm, about 30 seconds per side.

INDOOR
Preheat overhead grill. Grill, turning every 2 minutes, until well browned but still juicy and slightly pink inside, 8-10 minutes. Briefly warm pitta halves under the grill, about 15 seconds per side.

THINK AHEAD
Marinate lamb up to 1 day in advance. Cover and refrigerate.

LAMB TIKKA MASALA

SERVES 4

500g (1lb) boneless lamb, cut into 4cm (1½in) cubes
  (see page 58)
2 tbsp grated fresh ginger
4 garlic cloves, crushed
1 fresh green chilli, seeded and finely chopped
2 tbsp finely chopped fresh coriander
2 tbsp garam masala mix (see page 25)
1 tsp ground turmeric
2 tbsp red wine vinegar
150ml (5floz) greek-style yoghurt
20 fresh bay leaves
20 fresh whole green chillies
salt, black pepper
4 naan or other flat bread
1 recipe cucumber yoghurt raita (see page 138), optional

ESSENTIAL EQUIPMENT
4 – 35cm (14in) flat metal skewers

Combine lamb cubes, ginger, garlic, chilli, fresh coriander, masala mix, turmeric, vinegar and yoghurt. Toss well to coat evenly. Cover and refrigerate for 2 hours. Thread lamb cubes, bay leaves and chillies on to skewers. Grill lamb skewers and warm naan according to instructions below. Sprinkle with salt and pepper. Serve hot with warm naan and cucumber yoghurt raita, optional.

OUTDOOR
Grill over medium-hot coals, turning every 2 minutes, until well browned but still juicy and slightly pink inside, 8-10 minutes. Warm the naan by setting directly on the grill, 1 minute per side.

INDOOR
Preheat overhead grill. Grill, turning every 2 minutes, until well browned but still juicy and slightly pink inside, 8-10 minutes. Briefly warm the naan under the grill, 30 seconds per side.

THINK AHEAD
Marinate lamb cubes up to 1 day in advance. Cover and refrigerate.

SPICED COCONUT LAMB SATAYS

SERVES 4

500g (1lb) boneless lamb, cut into 4cm (1½in) cubes
  (see page 58)
1 onion, chopped
2 garlic cloves, crushed
2 fresh red chillies, seeded and chopped
1 tbsp grated fresh ginger
1 tsp ground coriander
1 tbsp tamarind paste or lime juice
3 tbsp coconut milk
1 tbsp soy sauce
1 tbsp dark brown sugar
salt, black pepper
1 recipe spicy peanut sauce (see page 136), optional

ESSENTIAL EQUIPMENT
4 – 35cm (14in) flat metal skewers

Place onion, garlic, chillies, ginger, coriander, tamarind or lime juice, coconut milk, soy sauce and sugar in food processor or blender; pulse to form a paste. In a bowl, combine paste with lamb cubes, tossing to coat evenly. Cover and refrigerate for 2 hours. Thread lamb on to skewers. Grill according to instructions below. Sprinkle with salt and pepper. Serve hot with spicy peanut sauce, optional.

OUTDOOR
Grill over medium-hot coals, turning every 2 minutes, until well browned but still juicy and slightly pink inside, 8-10 minutes.

INDOOR
Preheat overhead grill. Grill, turning every 2 minutes, until well browned but still juicy and slightly pink inside, 8-10 minutes.

THINK AHEAD
Marinate lamb up to 1 day in advance. Cover and refrigerate.

COOKS' NOTE
Dark, shiny tamarind paste - sometimes referred to as concentrate - has a refreshing, sharp citrus flavour. It is usually found in Asian and Middle-Eastern stores. If you can't find it, use tamarind pulp. For this recipe, dissolve 2 tbsp pulp in 4 tbsp boiling water, then cool and sieve before using. Alternatively, use lime juice.

HONEY HARISSA KOFTE

SERVES 4

500g (1lb) minced lamb
1 onion, grated
4 garlic cloves, crushed
2 tbsp finely chopped fresh mint
1 tbsp runny honey
1 tbsp tomato purée
3 tsp ground coriander
2 tsp ground cumin
1 tsp ground caraway seeds
1 tsp crushed chilli flakes
1½ tsp salt
½ tsp black pepper
1 recipe radish tzatziki (see page 135), optional

ESSENTIAL EQUIPMENT
8 – 25cm (10in) presoaked bamboo skewers

Place minced lamb, onion, garlic, mint, honey, tomato purée, coriander, cumin, caraway, chilli flakes, salt and pepper in a food processor; pulse until combined. Divide into 8 equal-sized portions. With wet hands, mould each portion round a separate skewer, shaping it into a sausage, about 15cm (6in) long. Grill according to instructions below. Sprinkle with salt and pepper. Serve hot with radish tzatziki, optional.

OUTDOOR
Grill over medium-hot coals, turning every 2 minutes, until well browned but still juicy and slightly pink inside, 8-10 minutes.

INDOOR
Preheat overhead grill. Grill, turning every 2 minutes, until well browned but still juicy and slightly pink inside, 8-10 minutes.

THINK AHEAD
Prepare and skewer kofte up to 1 day in advance. Cover with cling film and refrigerate.

CHARMOULA LAMB KOFTE

SERVES 4

500g (1lb) minced lamb
1 onion, grated
½ tsp black pepper
1½ tsp salt
1 recipe charmoula (see page 23)
1 recipe spiced chickpea sauce (see page 137), optional

ESSENTIAL EQUIPMENT
8 – 35cm (14in) flat metal skewers

Place lamb, onion, salt, black pepper and charmoula in a food processor; pulse until combined. Divide into 8 equal-sized portions. With wet hands, mould each portion round a separate skewer, shaping it into a sausage, about 15cm (6in) long. Grill according to instructions below. Sprinkle with salt and pepper. Serve hot with spiced chickpea sauce, optional.

OUTDOOR
Grill over medium-hot coals, turning every 2 minutes, until well browned but still juicy and slightly pink inside, 8-10 minutes.

INDOOR
Preheat overhead grill. Grill, turning every 2 minutes, until well browned but still juicy and slightly pink inside, 8-10 minutes.

THINK AHEAD
Prepare and skewer kofte up to 1 day in advance. Cover with cling film and refrigerate.

SKEWERING AND SLASHING FILLETS

Cut the neck fillets into four equal-sized pieces. Thread a skewer lengthwise through the middle of each piece.

With a sharp knife, make cuts approximately 2½ cm (1in) apart down the length of each skewered piece.

THINK AHEAD
Skewer and slash fillets up to 1 day in advance. Cover and refrigerate.

COOKS' NOTE
Slashing lamb ensures that the marinade will penetrate the meat completely, and that the meat will cook evenly.

SKEWERED CUMIN LAMB WITH GARLIC YOGHURT SAUCE

SERVES 4

500g (1lb) boned lamb neck fillets, skewered and slashed (see opposite)

FOR MARINADE
2 garlic cloves, crushed
2 tbsp cumin seeds, toasted and roughly pounded (see page 161)
½ tsp ground coriander
½ tsp crushed chilli flakes
1 tbsp lemon juice
1 tbsp olive oil

ESSENTIAL EQUIPMENT
4 – 25cm (10in) presoaked bamboo skewers

FOR SAUCE
2 whole unpeeled garlic heads
1 tbsp olive oil
salt, black pepper
2 tsp creamy dijon mustard
2 tbsp balsamic vinegar
2 tbsp double cream
1 handful flat-leaf parsley
150ml (5floz) greek-style yoghurt
salt, black pepper

For marinade, combine garlic, cumin, coriander, chilli flakes, lemon juice and oil. Rub over skewered lamb fillets. Cover and refrigerate for 1 hour. For sauce, preheat oven to 180°C (350°F) gas 4. Slice off top of both garlic heads, cutting through the tops of the cloves. Place cut-side up in oven tray. Drizzle over olive oil and sprinkle with salt and pepper. Roast until completely soft, 1 hour. Leave until cool enough to handle. Squeeze out cloves from papery skins into a food processor or blender. Add mustard, vinegar, cream, parsley and yoghurt; pulse until smooth. Add salt and pepper to taste. Grill lamb according to instructions below. Sprinkle lamb with salt and pepper. Serve hot with the garlic yoghurt sauce.

OUTDOOR
Grill over medium-hot coals, turning every 2 minutes, 8 minutes for medium rare, 12 minutes for well done.

INDOOR
Preheat a ridged cast iron grill pan over high heat. Grill, turning every 2 minutes, 8 minutes for medium rare, 12 minutes for well done.

THINK AHEAD
Make sauce up to 1 day in advance. Cover and refrigerate. Marinate lamb up to 1 day in advance. Cover and refrigerate.

COOKS' NOTE
Spiced chickpea sauce (see page 137) or radish tzatziki (see page 135) are excellent alternatives to the garlic yoghurt sauce served with this Middle-Eastern-spiced lamb dish.

SEAFOOD ON THE GRILL

PRAWNS WITH SALSA FRESCA

SERVES 4

1 recipe salsa fresca (see page 133)
375g (13oz) medium prawns, cooked
  and peeled
2 tbsp chopped fresh coriander

2 tbsp sour cream
salt, black pepper, tabasco
1 large bag plain, lightly salted
  tortilla chips

ESSENTIAL EQUIPMENT
heavy cast iron frying pan

Set dry pan over grill or stove as instructed below. When pan is hot, add salsa.
When salsa is bubbling add prawns and stir fry until prawns are hot, 1 minute.
Remove from heat. Stir in coriander and cream. Add salt, pepper and tabasco to
taste. Add a handful of tortilla chips. Serve hot, with extra tortilla chips and sour
cream for dipping.

OUTDOOR
On a charcoal grill, set pan over hot, flaming coals.

INDOOR
Set pan on stove over high heat.

SPICY MASALA PRAWNS

SERVES 4

4 tbsp garam masala mix
  (see page 25)
1 tsp chilli powder
2 tbsp paprika
2 tsp turmeric
1 tsp ground coriander
2 tsp salt
4 garlic cloves, crushed
1 tbsp grated fresh ginger
1 tbsp lemon juice
125g (4oz) butter, melted
20 raw unpeeled tiger prawns
lemon wedges

ESSENTIAL EQUIPMENT
20 - 25cm (10in) presoaked bamboo skewers

Combine garam masala mix, chilli
powder, paprika, turmeric, coriander,
salt, garlic, ginger, lemon juice and butter to make a paste. Rub paste
thoroughly into prawns to coat evenly.
Skewer each prawn on to the end of a
single skewer. Cover with cling film and
refrigerate for 30 minutes. Grill
according to instructions below. Serve
with lemon wedges.

OUTDOOR
Grill over medium-hot
coals until the shell is
pink and the flesh is
opaque, 3 minutes
per side.

INDOOR
Preheat overhead grill.
Grill until the shell is pink
and the flesh is opaque,
3 minutes per side.

THINK AHEAD
Rub prawns with paste up to 2 hours in advance.
Cover and refrigerate.

COOKS' NOTE
Use Kashmiri chilli powder for an authentically Indian
flavour and colour. This chilli powder is made from the
mildly spicy and pungent chillies that are traditionally
used in tandoori dishes.

SWEET SESAME PRAWNS

SERVES 4

1 tbsp sesame seeds
1 tbsp sesame oil
2 garlic cloves, crushed
1 tbsp soy sauce
1 tbsp mirin
20 raw tiger prawns, peeled
lime wedges

ESSENTIAL EQUIPMENT
4 - 25cm (10in) presoaked bamboo skewers

Combine sesame seeds, sesame oil, garlic, soy sauce and mirin. Add prawns and toss to coat evenly. Thread 5 prawns on to each presoaked skewer. Repeat with remaining prawns and skewers. Cover with cling film and refrigerate for 30 minutes. Grill according to instructions below. Serve with lime wedges.

OUTDOOR
Grill over medium-hot coals until the shell is pink and the flesh is opaque, 3 minutes per side.

INDOOR
Preheat overhead grill. Grill until the shell is pink and the flesh is opaque, 3 minutes per side.

THINK AHEAD
Marinate prawns up to 2 hours in advance. Cover and refrigerate.

LEMON CHILLI PRAWNS

SERVES 4

3 tbsp lemon juice
½ tbsp chinese hot chilli sauce
1 tbsp grated fresh ginger
2 garlic cloves, crushed

2 tbsp chopped fresh coriander
1 tbsp soy sauce
1 tbsp runny honey
20 raw unpeeled tiger prawns

ESSENTIAL EQUIPMENT
8 - 25cm (10in) presoaked bamboo skewers

Combine lemon juice, chilli sauce, ginger, garlic, coriander, soy sauce and honey. Add prawns and toss to coat evenly. Thread 5 prawns on to parallel skewers. Repeat with remaining prawns and skewers. Cover with cling film and refrigerate for 30 minutes. Grill according to instructions below.

OUTDOOR
Grill over medium-hot coals until the shell is pink and the flesh is opaque, 3 minutes per side.

INDOOR
Preheat overhead grill. Grill until the shell is pink and the flesh is opaque, 3 minutes per side.

THINK AHEAD
Marinate prawns up to 2 hours in advance. Cover and refrigerate.

PRAWNS WITH TAMARIND RECADO

SERVES 4

FOR RECADO
3 tbsp tamarind paste
1 chipotle in adobo, seeded and
   finely chopped
3 garlic cloves, crushed

ESSENTIAL EQUIPMENT
4 - 25cm (10in) presoaked bamboo skewers

1 tsp salt
1 tsp dark brown sugar
20 raw tiger prawns, peeled
1 recipe pineapple lime salsa
   (see page 134)

(see page 134)

For recado, combine tamarind paste, chipotle, garlic, salt and sugar. Add prawns and toss to coat evenly. Thread 5 prawns onto each presoaked skewer. Cover with cling film and refrigerate for 30 minutes. Grill according to instructions below. Serve with pineapple lime salsa.

OUTDOOR
Grill over medium-hot coals until the shell is pink and the flesh is opaque, 3 minutes per side.

INDOOR
Preheat overhead grill. Grill until the shell is pink and the flesh is opaque, 3 minutes per side.

THINK AHEAD
Marinate prawns up to 2 hours in advance. Cover and refrigerate.

COOKS' NOTE
Dark, shiny tamarind paste - sometimes referred to as concentrate - has a refreshing, sharp citrus flavour (see page 159). It can be found in most Asian and Middle-Eastern stores. If you can't find the paste, use tamarind pulp. For this recipe, dissolve 3 tbsp pulp in 3 tbsp boiling water, then cool and sieve before using.

PRAWN VARIATION
SPICY LIME PRAWNS

Omit tamarind recado and replace with 2 crushed garlic cloves, 1 tsp paprika, ½ tsp chilli powder, 1 tbsp lime juice, 1 tsp salt. Marinate, skewer and grill prawns according to recipe opposite. Serve with pineapple lime salsa or lime wedges.

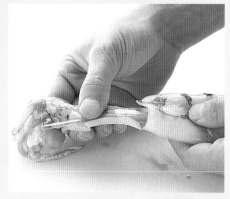

BABY SQUID STUFFED WITH CORIANDER AND PICKLED GINGER

SERVES 4

12 baby squid, about 7.5cm (3in) long, cleaned (see opposite)
1 tbsp shoyu (japanese soy sauce)
1 tbsp sunflower oil
½ tsp black pepper

12 pieces japanese pickled ginger
2 tbsp fresh coriander leaves
2 garlic cloves, finely sliced
extra shoyu to drizzle

ESSENTIAL EQUIPMENT
24 - 25cm (10in) presoaked bamboo skewers

Combine squid, shoyu, oil and pepper. Toss to coat evenly.
Place 1 piece pickled ginger, a few coriander leaves and 1 garlic slice inside each tube. Insert the tentacles into the tubes. Thread 2 skewers through each squid to secure tentacles to tubes. Grill according to instructions below. Drizzle with shoyu. Serve hot.

OUTDOOR
Grill over medium-hot coals until just opaque, 1-2 minutes per side.

INDOOR
Preheat a ridged cast iron grill pan over high heat. Grill until just opaque, 1-2 minutes per side.

THINK AHEAD
Prepare squid up to 2 hours in advance. Cover with cling film and refrigerate.

COOKS' NOTE
If you don't have pickled ginger, you can use fresh ginger instead. Grate a 1cm (½in) piece of ginger and divide evenly among squid tubes.

CLEANING SQUID
Pull the body from the head and tentacles. Pull out the plastic-like quill. Reserve body tube.

Cut the tentacles from the head in front of the eyes. Squeeze the "beak" from the tentacles and discard, reserving tentacles.

Peel the purple skin from the body tubes and tentacles. Wash the tubes under cold running water.

COOKS' NOTE
Cleaning squid may look daunting and messy, but it's a surprisingly quick and easy process.

BABY SQUID STUFFED WITH CORIANDER AND PICKLED GINGER

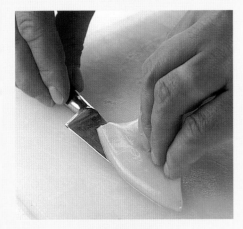

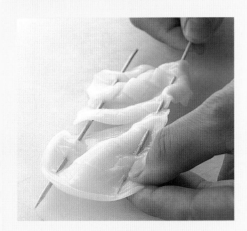

OPENING CLEANED SQUID TUBES
With a small, sharp knife, slit down one side of the tube and spread flat.

SCORING SQUID
Score inner side with parallel lines about 1cm (½in) apart to make cross hatch pattern.

SKEWERING SQUID
Cut squid into 7.5cm (3in) pieces. Thread strips across parallel skewers.

COOKS' NOTE
Squid needs to be cooked either very quickly over high heat or very slowly over low heat, to avoid a tough rubbery texture. When grilling squid, be sure to remove it from the grill as soon as it is done.

SQUID WITH TOMATO AVOCADO SALSA

SERVES 4

FOR SALSA

4 tomatoes, seeded and diced
1 avocado, diced
3 spring onions, finely chopped
1 fresh green chilli, seeded and finely chopped
1 tbsp finely chopped coriander
1 garlic clove, crushed

4 tbsp lime juice
3 tbsp olive oil

350g (12oz) large squid tubes, 25cm (10in) long, cleaned (see page 68)
1 tbsp olive oil
salt, black pepper

For salsa, combine tomatoes, avocado, spring onion, chilli, coriander, garlic, lime juice and oil. Add salt and pepper to taste.
Open and score squid tubes (see opposite). Toss in oil. Thread on to skewers (see opposite). Grill according to instructions below. Cut grilled squid into 1cm (½in) strips. Combine squid strips with salsa. Add salt and pepper to taste. Serve hot or at room temperature.

OUTDOOR
Grill over medium-hot coals until just opaque, 2 minutes per side.

INDOOR
Preheat a ridged cast iron grill pan over high heat. Grill until just opaque, 2 minutes per side.

THINK AHEAD
Make salsa up to 3 hours in advance. Cover tightly with cling film and refrigerate.

SPICY MARINATED SQUID ON BRUSCHETTA

SERVES 4

350g (12oz) large squid tubes, 25cm
  (10in) long, cleaned (see page 68)
1 tbsp olive oil
½ red onion, finely chopped
1 garlic clove, crushed
½ tsp crushed chilli flakes
2 tbsp olive oil

1 tbsp lemon juice
2 tomatoes, seeded and diced
1 tbsp chopped fresh mint
salt, black pepper
8 - 1cm (½in) thick slices of day-old
  ciabatta or country-style bread

ESSENTIAL EQUIPMENT
8 – 25cm (10in) presoaked bamboo skewers

Open and score squid tubes (see page 69). Toss squid in 1 tbsp olive oil and skewer
(see page 69). Grill squid according to instructions below. Cut grilled squid into 1cm
(½in) wide strips. Combine onion, garlic, chilli flakes, olive oil, lemon juice, tomatoes
and mint in a bowl. Add squid and toss to coat evenly. Leave at room temperature
for 30 minutes. Toast bread until crisp and striped, 2 minutes per side. Top with
squid. Serve at room temperature or chilled.

OUTDOOR
Grill over medium-hot coals until just opaque,
1-2 minutes per side.

INDOOR
Preheat a ridged cast iron grill pan over high heat.
Grill until just opaque, 1-2 minutes per side.

THINK AHEAD
Grill and marinate squid up to 1 day in advance. Cover and refrigerate.

LEMON CHARMOULA SQUID

SERVES 4

350g (12oz) large squid tubes, 25cm
  (10in) long, cleaned (see page 68)
1 tbsp olive oil
1 recipe charmoula (see page 23)
1 lemon, peeled and chopped
  (see page 161)
salt, black pepper

ESSENTIAL EQUIPMENT
16 - 25cm (10in) presoaked bamboo skewers

Open and score squid tubes (see page
69). Cut scored tubes in to 6 pieces. Toss
in olive oil. Thread on to parallel skewers (see page 69), with 3 pieces per pair
of skewers. Grill according to instructions below. Combine charmoula with
lemon. Toss squid with charmoula and
lemon to coat. Sprinkle with salt and
pepper. Serve hot, at room temperature,
or chilled.

OUTDOOR
Grill over medium-hot
coals until just opaque,
2 minutes per side.

INDOOR
Preheat a ridged cast iron
grill pan over high heat.
Grill until just opaque,
2 minutes per side.

THINK AHEAD
Grill squid and combine with charmoula and lemon
up to 1 day in advance. Cover and refrigerate.

COOKS' NOTE
For an authentic Moroccan flavour, use 1 finely
chopped preserved lemon in place of the fresh lemon.
Preserved lemons are available from Middle-Eastern
and gourmet stores (see page 167).

CUTTING A LOBSTER IN HALF
Place the lobster belly side down. Insert the tip of a large knife at the cross mark right behind the head and cut through the head (see above). Turn the lobster round. Holding it firmly by the head, cut it in half lengthwise from head to tail.

CHARGRILLED LOBSTER WITH GARLIC PARSLEY BUTTER

SERVES 4

**4 large cooked lobsters
125g (4oz) garlic parsley butter (see page 140), melted
lemon wedges**

Cut lobster in half with a large sharp knife (see opposite). Scoop out the head sac and discard. Grill according to instructions below. Serve warm with lemon wedges and remaining butter drizzled over.

OUTDOOR
Grill shell side down over medium-hot coals, frequently brushing flesh with butter, until warmed through, 5 minutes.

INDOOR
Preheat overhead grill. Grill flesh side up, brushing with butter, until warmed through, 5 minutes.

THINK AHEAD
Split lobsters up to 2 hours in advance. Cover and refrigerate.

COOKS' NOTE
Coriander chilli butter (see page 140) in place of the garlic parsley butter, and lime wedges in place of lemon wedges make an excellent alternative recipe for this grilled lobster.

FLAME-ROAST LOBSTER

SERVES 4

**4 large cooked lobsters
1 recipe roast garlic aïoli (see page 143)
lemon wedges**

OUTDOOR
Grill whole lobster over medium coals until hot to the touch, 5 minutes per side. Bash open and serve warm with roast garlic aïoli and lemon wedges.

CLAMS IN CORIANDER CHILLI BUTTER

SERVES 4
2kg (4lb) clams
125g (4oz) coriander chilli butter (see page 140), melted

Scrub clams under running water. Discard any that are broken or not tightly closed. To cook outdoors, fold 1 metre of foil in half for double thickness. Spread clams over middle of foil. Fold in the edges to make a parcel. To cook indoors, put clams in a large dry pan and cover. Grill or cook according to instructions below. Pour over the melted butter and remove from the heat when butter is hot and fragrant, 1 minute. Serve hot, discarding any clams that have not opened.

OUTDOOR
Grill over medium-low coals until shells are open and the clams turn opaque, 8-10 minutes. Open the foil out but leave the edges raised so that no juices escape.

INDOOR
Cook over medium heat until shells open and the clams turn opaque, 6 minutes. Shake pan occasionally to ensure even cooking.

MUSSELS IN BEER AND GARLIC

SERVES 4
2kg (4lb) mussels
100ml (3½ floz) lager
2 garlic cloves, finely chopped
2 tbsp chopped flat-leaf parsley
salt, black pepper

Scrub mussels under running water. Discard any that are broken or not tightly closed. To cook outdoors, fold 1 metre of foil in half for double thickness. Spread mussels over middle of foil. Scrunch up the edges of the foil and pour over the lager. Fold up edges to make a parcel. To cook indoors, put mussels and lager in a large pan with a lid on. Grill or cook according to instructions below. Sprinkle with the garlic and parsley. Remove from heat when you can smell the garlic, 1 minute. Sprinkle with salt and pepper. Serve hot, discarding any mussels that have not opened.

OUTDOOR
Grill over medium-low coals until shells are open and the mussels turn opaque, 8-10 minutes. Open the foil but leave the edges raised so no juices escape.

INDOOR
Steam over medium heat until shells are open and the mussels turn opaque, 6 minutes. Shake pan occasionally to ensure even cooking.

FISH ESSENTIALS

GOLDEN RULE FOR COOKING FISH
Never desert your post once fish is placed on the grill. Fish is naturally tender. Most fish requires only brief grilling to firm its flesh and to bring out its delicate flavour. Overcooked fish is dry and tasteless, and overcooking can happen in a matter of minutes.

SELECTING FISH FOR THE GRILL
• Oil rich fish with a firm meaty texture is the easiest to grill. This includes salmon, tuna, halibut, swordfish, snapper and mackerel.
• Skin left on fish acts to protect the delicate flesh and turns deliciously crisp on the grill.
• Firm textured flesh also means that the fish will hold together better.

GETTING IT READY
• Cut deep slashes through the skin side of fish fillets and through to the bone of whole fish to allow flavour, smoke and heat to penetrate evenly.
• Liberal oiling is important for all types of fish to prevent it from drying out, except in the case of very oily skinned fish, like sardines.

MARINATING
• Fish requires only a very brief amount of time in a marinade. Tender fish flesh absorbs a marinade faster than the denser flesh of red meat. When left in an acidic marinade for too long, fish flesh will literally start to cook and turn white.

• Marinate fish for no longer than 2 hours in the refrigerator. It is better to drizzle or brush an oil rich flavour mix over the fish flesh than give it a long soak in a wet acidic marinade.

PUTTING IT ON
• Before putting fish on the grill make sure to bring it to room temperature. Remove it from the refrigerator no more than 30 minutes beforehand. This will ensure that it cooks evenly and quickly.
• Use a hinged grill rack to turn fish that is tender and delicate. It will help to keep whole fish intact and prevent fillets from breaking apart.
• When turning fish with a metal spatula, turn only once, to stop the fish from falling apart.

TAKING IT OFF
Fish will continue cooking a significant amount after it is removed from the grill. To avoid overcooked, dry and flavourless fish, remove as soon as it is done. You can always put it back on but once it is overcooked there is no quick fix. Fish is done when it is opaque through to the centre but still moist and tender. Cook fish until the internal temperature reads 60°C (140°F).

FINAL FLAVOURING
• Salting raw fish draws out moisture and toughens the flesh. Always add seasoning after cooking but be sure not to forget.

• Add complementary flavours and moisture after removing it from the grill with sauces, salsas and dressings (consult pages 130-143 for more ideas).

CHARGRILLED SWORDFISH WITH ROAST PEPPER AND BASIL SALSA

SERVES 4

4 -175g (6oz) swordfish steaks
1 tbsp olive oil
salt, black pepper

1 recipe roast pepper and basil salsa (see page 138)

ESSENTIAL EQUIPMENT
hinged wire rack, or alternatively a long metal spatula for turning fish on the grill

Brush the steaks with olive oil on both sides. Grill according to instructions below. Sprinkle with salt and pepper. Spoon over salsa and serve hot.

OUTDOOR
Grill over medium-hot coals until just opaque, 3 minutes per side.

INDOOR
Preheat a ridged cast iron grill pan over high heat. Grill until just opaque, 3 minutes per side.

COOKS' NOTE
Salsa fresca (see page 133), coriander coconut sauce (see page 138), salsa verde (see page 134) and chilli lime mayonnaise (see page 143) all complement swordfish wonderfully. Shark, salmon, halibut or monkfish make excellent alternatives to swordfish with this simple, no-frills preparation.

SPICE-CRUSTED TUNA WITH THAI CITRUS DRESSING

SERVES 4

4 - 200g (7oz) tuna fillets, 2.5cm (1in) thick
1 tbsp sunflower oil
2 tbsp coriander seeds
2 tbsp black peppercorns
lime wedges

FOR DRESSING
2 lemon grass stalks
1 fresh red chilli, seeded and finely sliced
1 tbsp finely chopped fresh coriander
2 tbsp fish sauce
2 tbsp sunflower oil
6 tbsp lime juice

ESSENTIAL EQUIPMENT
hinged wire rack, or alternatively a long metal spatula for turning fish on the grill

For dressing, remove and discard the tough outer skin from the lemon grass stalks and finely slice. Combine lemon grass, chilli, fresh coriander, fish sauce, oil and lime juice. Brush fillets on both sides with oil. Crush the coriander seeds and peppercorns (see page 161). Press crushed seeds on to both sides of fillets. Grill according to instructions below. Pour over dressing and serve hot or at room temperature with lime wedges.

OUTDOOR
Grill over hot coals, 2 minutes per side for rare, 3 minutes per side for medium rare, 4 minutes per side for well done.

INDOOR
Preheat a ridged cast iron grill pan over high heat. Grill for 2 minutes per side for rare, 3 minutes per side for medium rare, 4 minutes per side for well done.

THINK AHEAD
Coat tuna with spices up to 4 hours in advance. Cover and refrigerate. Make dressing up to 3 hours in advance. Cover and refrigerate.

COOKS' NOTE
Salsa fresca (see page 133), creamy avocado salsa (see page 132), roast pepper and basil salsa (see page 138), or avocado mango salsa (see page 136) are all delicious served with this simple tuna recipe.

CHARGRILLED SARDINES

SERVES 4

24 - 30g (1oz) ungutted small sardines
salt, black pepper

ESSENTIAL EQUIPMENT
hinged wire rack

Grill sardines according to instructions below. Sprinkle with salt and pepper. Serve hot with lemon wedges.

OUTDOOR
Place sardines in hinged wire rack. Grill over medium-hot coals until opaque throughout and crispy on the outside, 3 minutes per side.

INDOOR
Don't even attempt to grill sardines indoors, unless you are planning to move house. The aroma will linger forever!

COOKS' NOTE
If you grill large sardines they will need cleaning and gutting. Allow 3 sardines per person. Grill for 5 minutes per side.

CHARGRILLED SEA BASS WITH FENNEL, LEMON AND OLIVE OIL

SERVES 4

4 - 175g (6oz) unskinned sea bass
  fillets
1 fennel bulb, grated
4 garlic cloves, finely sliced
2 tbsp chopped flat-leaf parsley
1½ tsp salt
1 tsp black pepper
1 tsp fennel seeds
1 tbsp olive oil
1 lemon, sliced
1 recipe salsa verde (see page 134),
  optional

ESSENTIAL EQUIPMENT
4 – 40cm (16in) squares heavy duty foil

Cut several shallow diagonal slashes about 2.5cm (1in) apart on the skin side of each fillet. Divide the fennel, garlic and parsley among the foil squares, spreading in an even layer on one half of each foil piece. Place the fish skin side up on top. Sprinkle with salt, pepper and fennel seeds. Drizzle over oil. Place lemon slices on top. Fold over the other half of the foil. Fold over edges to seal foil packets tightly. Grill or bake according to instructions below. Serve hot in foil packet with salsa verde.

OUTDOOR
Grill over medium-hot coals until fish is opaque throughout, 8-10 minutes. Flip foil packet over half way through grilling.

INDOOR
Preheat oven to 200°C (400°F) gas 6. Bake until fish is opaque throughout, 8-10 minutes

THINK AHEAD
Prepare foil packets up to 2 hours in advance. Refrigerate.

COOKS' NOTE
Sea bream, grey mullet, grouper or red snapper fillets make good alternatives to sea bass in this fennel-fragrant recipe.

HERBED SALMON WITH TOMATO VINAIGRETTE

SERVES 4

2 - 350g (12oz) tail end salmon fillets
juice of 1 lemon
2 tbsp finely chopped fresh dill
2 tsp salt
1 tsp black pepper
½ tsp coriander seeds, crushed
  (see page 161)

ESSENTIAL EQUIPMENT
hinged grill rack

FOR VINAIGRETTE
1 garlic clove, crushed
1 shallot, finely chopped
2 tbsp red wine vinegar
4 tbsp olive oil
3 tomatoes, seeded and diced
salt, black pepper

For vinaigrette, combine garlic, shallot and vinegar. Leave to stand for 30 minutes. Whisk in the oil and tomatoes. Add salt and pepper to taste. Place salmon fillets skin side down. Drizzle lemon juice evenly over both fillets. Sprinkle 1 salmon fillet with dill, salt, pepper and coriander seeds. Place uncoated fillet skin side up over the other fillet. Grill according to instructions below. Cut into four portions. Spoon over vinaigrette and serve hot.

OUTDOOR
Place sandwiched fillets in hinged grill rack. Grill over medium-hot coals until skin is very crisp and flesh has just turned opaque but is still moist and pink in the centre, 5 minutes per side.

INDOOR
Preheat oven to 200°C (400°F) gas 6. Place sandwiched fillets on rack in roasting tin. Roast until flesh has just turned opaque but is still moist and pink in the centre, 15-20 minutes.

THINK AHEAD
Sandwich fillets together up to 2 hours in advance. Cover tightly with cling film and refrigerate. Make vinaigrette up to 6 hours in advance. Cover and refrigerate.

MOROCCAN SPICED MACKEREL

SERVES 4

4 - 375g (13oz) whole mackerel
1 recipe charmoula (see page 23)
salt, black pepper

ESSENTIAL EQUIPMENT
hinged wire rack, or alternatively a long metal spatula for turning fish on the grill

Cut slashes about 5cm (2in) apart down both sides of each fish, cutting through to the bones. Spread ½ tbsp of the charmoula down both sides of the inside cavity of each fish. Grill according to instructions below. Sprinkle with salt and pepper. Serve hot with the remaining charmoula.

OUTDOOR
Grill over medium-hot coals until flesh is opaque at the bone and skin is very crispy, 5 minutes per side.

INDOOR
Preheat overhead grill. Grill until the flesh is opaque at the bone and the skin is very crispy, 5 minutes per side.

THINK AHEAD
Prepare mackerel for grilling up to 2 hours in advance. Cover tightly with cling film and refrigerate.

COOKS' NOTE
Chimi churri sauce (see page 135) used as an alternative to the charmoula is also very good for flavouring mackerel.

WASABI SOY SALMON WITH SESAME SOBA NOODLES

SERVES 4

4 -175g (6oz) salmon fillets
1 tsp wasabi paste
2 tsp brown sugar
1 tbsp sake

1 tbsp lime juice
3 tbsp shoyu (japanese soy sauce)
1 recipe sesame soba noodle salad
(see page 148)

ESSENTIAL EQUIPMENT
hinged wire rack, or alternatively a long metal spatula for turning fish on the grill

Combine wasabi, sugar, sake, lime and shoyu. Set aside 2 tbsp for drizzling. Brush the fillets on both sides with the remaining mixture. Grill according to instructions below. Serve hot with sesame soba noodle salad and drizzle over reserved mixture.

OUTDOOR
Grill over medium-hot coals until the flesh just turns opaque but is still moist and pink in the middle, 3-4 minutes per side.

INDOOR
Preheat a ridged cast iron grill pan over high heat. Grill until the flesh just turns opaque but is still moist and pink in the middle, 3-4 minutes per side.

THINK AHEAD
Brush the salmon up to 30 minutes in advance.

CHARGRILLED TROUT WITH GARLIC PARSLEY BUTTER

SERVES 4

4 - 250g (8oz) trout without head, butterflied (see opposite)
1 tbsp sunflower oil
salt, black pepper
lemon wedges
4 - 1cm (½in) slices garlic parsley butter (see page 140)

ESSENTIAL EQUIPMENT
hinged wire rack, or alternatively a long metal spatula for turning fish on the grill

Brush flesh side of trout with oil. Place trout in hinged wire rack, if using. Grill according to instructions below. Sprinkle with salt and pepper. Serve hot with garlic parsley butter and lemon wedges.

OUTDOOR
Grill skin side down over medium-hot coals until skin starts to turn crisp, 2 minutes. Turn and grill for 1 minute. Turn again. Grill until flesh just turns opaque, is firm, and the skin is crispy, a further 2 minutes.

INDOOR
Preheat overhead grill. Grill skin side up until skin starts to turn crispy, 2 minutes. Turn and grill for 1 minute. Turn again. Grill until flesh just turns opaque, is firm, and the skin is crispy, a further 2 minutes.

THINK AHEAD
Butterfly trout up to 8 hours in advance. Cover tightly with cling film and refrigerate.

BUTTERFLYING TROUT
Lay a gutted, headless trout skin side down on a cutting board. Working down one side, slide the tip of a sharp knife between the rib bones and flesh. Use small stroking cuts to release the bones. Repeat on the opposite side.

Place fish skin side down and open flat. Lift up backbone from head to tail and cut off with scissors.

RED SNAPPER TACOS WITH CHILLI LIME MAYO

SERVES 4

4 - 175g (6oz) unskinned red snapper
   fillets
1 garlic clove, crushed
½ tsp ground cumin
½ tsp chilli powder
½ tsp dried oregano
1 tbsp lime juice
2 tbsp olive oil
salt, black pepper
4 - 20cm (8in) flour tortillas or fresh
   corn tortillas
1 avocado, diced
2 tbsp fresh coriander leaves
1 recipe chilli lime mayonnaise
   (see page 143)

ESSENTIAL EQUIPMENT
*hinged wire rack, or alternatively a long metal
spatula for turning fish on the grill*

Combine the garlic, cumin, chilli powder,
oregano, lime juice and oil. Brush
mixture over fillets. Place fillets in
hinged wire rack, if using. Grill fillets
according to instructions below. Sprinkle
with salt and pepper. Warm tortillas
directly over the grill or in the hot grill
pan for 30 seconds each side. Cut fish
into 4cm (1½in) cubes. Divide among
warmed tortillas. Top with avocado dice,
coriander leaves and chilli lime
mayonnaise. Fold in half and serve hot.

OUTDOOR
Grill fillets over medium-
hot coals, skin side down
for 3 minutes. Turn and
grill until opaque
throughout, a further
3 minutes.

INDOOR
Preheat a ridged cast iron
grill pan. Grill fillets skin
side down for 3 minutes.
Turn and grill until
opaque throughout, a
further 3 minutes.

THINK AHEAD
Brush the snapper with seasoning up to 30 minutes
in advance.

COOKS' NOTE
Red mullet, grouper or sea bass fillets are excellent
alternatives to red snapper.

ALTERNATIVE SEAFOOD FOR
PROVENÇAL GRILLADE

ALTERNATIVE SEAFOOD FOR
PROVENÇAL GRILLADE

Feel free to make any of the
following substitutions:

4 cooked, cracked lobster claws, in
place of crab.

2 - 175g (6oz) fillets red snapper,
grouper or bass, in place of red and
grey mullet fillets.

2 - 175 (6oz) salmon or swordfish
steaks, in place of tuna.

12 tiger prawns, in place of
langoustine.

8 skewered scallops, grilled until just
opaque, 2 minutes per side, as an
optional addition.

PROVENÇAL SEAFOOD GRILLADE WITH LEMON FENNEL DRESSING AND ROAST GARLIC AÏOLI

SERVES 4 - 6

2 garlic cloves, crushed
2 tbsp pernod
2 tbsp olive oil
4 large cooked crab
500g (1lb) tuna fillet,
  2.5cm (1in) thick
2 - 175g (6oz) red mullet fillets
2 - 175g (6oz) grey mullet fillets
8 cooked langoustines

ESSENTIAL EQUIPMENT
long metal spatula

FOR DRESSING
6 tbsp olive oil
2 tbsp lemon juice
2 tbsp red wine vinegar
1 tbsp finely chopped fresh fennel
  or dill
salt, black pepper

1 recipe roast garlic aïoli
  (see page 143)
crusty bread and lemon wedges

For dressing, whisk oil into lemon and vinegar. Stir in fennel or dill. Add salt and pepper to taste. Combine garlic, pernod and oil. Using a hammer or rolling pin, crack crab or lobster claws just enough to expose the interior to seasoning. Brush all the seafood with the garlic mixture. Grill according to instructions below. Cut cooked tuna and fish fillets into chunks. Arrange seafood on platter. Drizzle over dressing. Serve hot or at room temperature with roast garlic aïoli, crusty bread and lemon wedges.

OUTDOOR
Grill seafood over medium-hot coals, using spatula to turn. Grill tuna for 3 minutes per side for rare, 4 minutes per side for medium rare, 5 minutes per side for well done. Grill fish fillets, skin side down first, until opaque throughout, 3 minutes per side. Grill shellfish until warmed through, 3 minutes per side.

INDOOR
This recipe is inappropriate for indoor cooking.

THINK AHEAD
Crack and brush seafood up to 2 hours in advance. Cover with cling film and refrigerate.

CHICKEN ON THE GRILL

CHICKEN ESSENTIALS

GETTING IT READY

Chicken should be grilled in pieces of uniform shape and thickness. This is essential to ensure safe, even cooking, and to guarantee the best results.

• De-boning joints (see page 104), splitting and flattening whole birds (see page 110) and butterflying boneless breasts (see page 94) allow chicken to cook evenly and prevent overcooked white meat.

• Slashing (see page 102) and making shallow cuts (see page 92) open the greatest surface area to flavour, smoke and heat. This allows marinades to penetrate more deeply and chicken to cook quickly and evenly.

MARINATING

The intense heat of an outdoor grill can dry out naturally lean chicken meat, especially when it has been de-boned and skinned. Marinating is an essential step to retaining moisture during cooking, but it is also important not to overdo it. Overmarinating will draw moisture out from, toughen, and when acid is present, literally begin to cook the meat. The result is poultry that looks greyish white and rubbery. Marinate for the recommended time only.

PUTTING IT ON

Before putting chicken on the grill make sure to bring it to room temperature, by removing it from the refrigerator no more than 20 minutes beforehand. This will ensure that it cooks evenly and quickly.

Be sure to brush poultry liberally with oil to keep it moist during grilling.

Cooking chicken for a crowd? Get ahead by pre-cooking on the bone chicken pieces (such as wings, drums and whole split birds) in a preheated 200°C (400°F) Gas 6 oven for 15 minutes. Transfer to the grill when your guests arrive and reduce the required cooking time by approximately 10 minutes.

TAKING IT OFF

Check doneness by making a cut into the meat with a small, sharp knife (see page 13), before removing chicken from the grill. It is always better to check doneness at the grill than to discover undercooked meat on the plate. Chicken is done when it is opaque throughout with no trace of pink at the bone.

Watch boneless cuts carefully to avoid overcooking and to ensure maximum juiciness and succulence.

FINAL FLAVOURING

We add salt just before serving because salting any sooner will draw out the chicken's flavourful juices. But don't forget to season before putting food on the table.

SAFETY TIPS FOR CHICKEN

The raw juices of uncooked chicken contain bacteria that can easily contaminate the cooked meat and other foods you are preparing. For healthy eating, be sure to take the following precautions:

• Always wash hands with soap and hot water before and after handling uncooked chicken.

• Never leave uncooked chicken at room temperature for more than 20 minutes.

• Never re-use a chicken marinade or baste cooked chicken with a marinade after it has been used.

• Never put cooked chicken back into the unwashed container in which it was marinating.

SLASHING CHICKEN BREASTS

With a sharp knife, cut 3 parallel slashes through skin, about 0.5cm (¼ in) deep.

COOKS' NOTE

We slash the chicken breasts to allow the flavours of the seasonings and marinades to penetrate the chicken more fully.

CITRUS RECADO CHICKEN BREASTS

SERVES 4

2 garlic cloves, crushed
1 tsp chilli powder
½ tsp dried oregano
½ tsp dried thyme
½ tsp ground cumin
½ tsp ground coriander
½ tsp black pepper
¼ tsp ground cinnamon
1 tbsp dark brown sugar

2 tbsp sunflower oil
2 tbsp lime juice
4 tbsp orange juice
4 boneless chicken breasts, slashed
  (see opposite)
salt
1 recipe avocado mango salsa
  (see page 136), optional

Combine garlic, chilli powder, oregano, thyme, cumin, coriander, pepper, cinnamon, sugar, oil, lime juice and orange juice. Add chicken and toss to coat evenly. Cover and refrigerate for 30 minutes, turning once. Grill according to instructions below. Sprinkle with salt. Serve hot with avocado mango salsa, optional.

OUTDOOR

Grill skin side down over medium-hot coals until skin is crisp, 7 minutes. Turn and continue grilling until chicken is opaque with no trace of pink, a further 5 minutes.

INDOOR

Preheat overhead grill. Grill skin side up until skin is crisp, 7 minutes. Turn and continue grilling until chicken is opaque with no trace of pink, a further 5 minutes.

THINK AHEAD

Marinate chicken up to 2 hours in advance. Cover and refrigerate, turning several times in marinade.

COOKS' NOTE

We prefer the mildly spicy sweet heat of ancho chilli powder in this Mexican-style dish. These wrinkled reddish brown chillies are actually dried poblanos. They are widely used in Mexican cooking. For complete authenticity, also try to find dried Mexican oregano. Both are available from speciality shops or gourmet mail order sources (see page 167).

HERBED BALSAMIC CHICKEN BREASTS

SERVES 4

2 garlic cloves, crushed
1 tsp herbes de provence
½ tsp black pepper
1 tbsp creamy dijon mustard
1 tbsp olive oil
4 tbsp balsamic vinegar
salt, black pepper
4 boneless chicken breasts, slashed (see page 92)
1 recipe roast red pepper aïoli (see page 143), optional

Combine garlic, herbes de provence, pepper, mustard, oil and vinegar. Add chicken and toss to coat evenly. Cover and refrigerate for 30 minutes, turning once. Grill according to instructions below. Sprinkle with salt and pepper. Serve hot with roast red pepper aïoli, optional.

OUTDOOR
Grill skin side down on medium-hot coals until crisp, 7 minutes. Turn and continue grilling until chicken is opaque with no trace of pink, a further 5 minutes.

INDOOR
Preheat overhead grill. Grill skin side up until skin is crisp, about 7 minutes. Turn and continue grilling until chicken is opaque with no trace of pink, a further 5 minutes.

THINK AHEAD
Marinate chicken breasts up to 2 hours in advance. Cover and refrigerate, turning every 15 to 20 minutes.

COOKS' NOTE
Herbes de Provence, a fragrant dry herb mix that includes fennel, lavender and summer savoury, is a kitchen cupboard essential. Sprinkle over poultry, meats, fish or vegetables to bring the scent and flavour of sun-soaked Provence into your kitchen.

GINGER SOY CHICKEN BREASTS

SERVES 4

2 tbsp grated fresh ginger
3 garlic cloves, crushed
2 tbsp dark brown sugar
2 tsp sesame seeds
2 tsp toasted sesame oil
1 tbsp medium dry sherry
8 tbsp soy sauce
4 boneless chicken breasts, slashed (see page 92)
salt, black pepper
1 recipe coriander coconut sauce (see page 138), optional

Combine ginger, garlic, sugar, sesame seeds, sesame oil, sherry and soy sauce. Add chicken and toss to coat evenly. Cover and refrigerate for 30 minutes, turning once. Grill according to instructions below. Sprinkle with salt and pepper. Serve hot with coriander coconut sauce, optional.

OUTDOOR
Grill skin side down on medium-hot coals until crisp, 7 minutes. Turn and continue grilling until chicken is opaque with no trace of pink, a further 5 minutes.

INDOOR
Preheat overhead grill. Grill skin side up until skin is crisp, 7 minutes. Turn and continue grilling until chicken is opaque with no trace of pink, a further 5 minutes.

THINK AHEAD
Marinate chicken breasts up to 2 hours in advance. Cover and refrigerate, turning every 15-20 minutes.

BUTTERFLYING CHICKEN BREAST
With one hand on the breast to hold it in place, slice through the middle horizontally to cut almost in half. Open out flat.

THINK AHEAD
Butterfly breast up to 1 day in advance. Cover tightly with cling film and refrigerate.

COOKS' NOTE
Butterflying makes chicken breasts into thin fillets that can be cooked in a flash. It also produces the perfect pocket for stuffing.

THAI LIME AND COCONUT CHICKEN

SERVES 4

2 lemon grass stalks
3 fresh green chillies, seeded and chopped
2 garlic cloves, chopped
3 spring onions, chopped
1 handful fresh coriander leaves
½ tsp ground cumin
½ tsp ground white pepper
½ tsp turmeric
1 tsp ground coriander

grated zest 1 lime
3 tbsp lime juice
2 tsp grated fresh ginger
1 tbsp fish sauce
125ml (4floz) coconut milk
4 boneless, skinless chicken breasts, butterflied (see opposite)
salt, black pepper
1 recipe fresh papaya sambal (see page 137), optional

Remove and discard the tough outer skin from the lemon grass stalks and roughly chop. Put lemon grass, chillies, garlic, spring onion, fresh coriander, cumin, pepper, turmeric, ground coriander, lime zest, lime juice, ginger, fish sauce and coconut milk in food processor or blender; pulse until smooth. In a bowl, toss chicken with lemon grass mixture. Cover and refrigerate for 1 hour. Grill according to instructions below. Sprinkle with salt and pepper. Serve hot with fresh papaya sambal, optional.

OUTDOOR
Grill over medium hot coals until the chicken is opaque, with no trace of pink, 3 minutes per side.

INDOOR
Preheat overhead grill. Grill until the chicken is opaque with no trace of pink, 3 minutes per side.

THINK AHEAD
Make marinade up to 3 days in advance. Cover and refrigerate. Marinate chicken up to 4 hours in advance. Cover and refrigerate.

LEMON OREGANO CHICKEN BAGUETTE

SERVES 4

4 boneless, skinless chicken breasts, butterflied (see page 94)
1 lemon, peeled and chopped (see page 161)
2 garlic cloves, crushed
2 tsp dried oregano
2 tbsp olive oil

1 tsp black pepper
1 baguette
salt
1 beefsteak tomato, sliced
1 handful crisp salad leaves
1 recipe roast garlic aïoli (see page 143)

Toss chicken breasts with lemon, garlic, oregano, oil and pepper. Cover and refrigerate for 20 minutes. Cut baguette into 4 equal-sized pieces. Split and toast baguette on the cut side until just crisp, 1 minute. Grill chicken according to instructions below. Sprinkle with salt. Fill baguette with tomatoes, salad, chicken and aïoli. Serve warm.

OUTDOOR
Grill over medium hot coals until chicken is opaque, with no trace of pink, 3 minutes per side.

INDOOR
Preheat overhead grill. Grill until the chicken is opaque with no trace of pink, 3 minutes per side.

THINK AHEAD
Marinate chicken up to 2 hours in advance. Cover and refrigerate, turning in the marinade every 15-20 minutes.

SKEWERED BAJUN CHICKEN

SERVES 4

2 garlic cloves
4 spring onions
½ red onion
½ scotch bonnet chilli, seeded or
  1 fresh red chilli, seeded
1 handful flat-leaf parsley
1 tsp fresh thyme leaves
2 tbsp lime juice

2 tbsp sunflower oil
¼ tsp ground allspice
salt, black pepper
4 boneless chicken breasts,
  butterflied (see page 94)
1 recipe creamy avocado salsa (see
  page 132), optional

ESSENTIAL EQUIPMENT
4 - 25cm (10in) presoaked bamboo skewers

Place garlic, spring onion, red onion, chilli, parsley, thyme, lime juice, oil and allspice in a food processor or blender; pulse to a paste. Add salt and pepper to taste. Open out chicken breasts and spread 1 tbsp paste on each opened breast. Fold breasts over again. Thread a skewer through cut edges of breast, weaving in and out several times to hold the chicken edges together. Grill according to instructions below. Sprinkle with salt and pepper. Serve hot with creamy avocado salsa, optional.

OUTDOOR
Grill skin side down over medium-hot coals until skin is crisp, 7 minutes. Turn and continue grilling until chicken is opaque with no trace of pink, a further 5 minutes.

INDOOR
Preheat overhead grill. Grill skin side up until skin is crisp, 7 minutes. Turn and continue grilling until chicken is opaque with no trace of pink, a further 5 minutes.

THINK AHEAD
Stuff breasts up to 1 day in advance. Wrap in cling film and refrigerate.

COOKS' NOTE
Butterflying breast produces a perfect pocket for stuffing. As an alternative to bajun stuffing, substitute charmoula (see page 23), spicy jerk rub (see page 24) or the simple combination of crushed garlic and chopped fresh herbs.

CHICKEN, PROSCIUTTO AND SAGE SKEWERS

SERVES 4

4 boneless, skinless chicken breasts
1 garlic clove, crushed
1 tsp black pepper
2 tbsp lemon juice
2 tbsp olive oil
6 slices prosciutto, cut in half
12 fresh sage leaves
4 - 2.5cm (1in) cubes country style
  day-old bread
1 recipe roast red pepper aïoli
  (see page 143)

ESSENTIAL EQUIPMENT
4 - 35cm (14in) flat metal skewers

Cut each breast lengthwise into 3 strips. Combine garlic, pepper, lemon and oil. Add chicken strips and toss to coat evenly. Place one sage leaf on top of each prosciutto half slice. Place one chicken strip on top of the sage. Roll up proscuitto and sage around each chicken strip. Thread 3 wrapped strips lengthwise on to each skewer. Toss bread cubes in 1 tbsp olive oil. Thread 1 bread cube on to the end of each skewer. Grill according to instructions below. Serve hot with roast red pepper aïoli.

OUTDOOR
Grill over medium-hot coals, turning every 2 minutes, until cooked through, 8-10 minutes.

INDOOR
Preheat overhead grill. Grill, turning every 2 minutes, until cooked through, 8-10 minutes.

THINK AHEAD
Skewer chicken but not bread up to 6 hours in advance. Cover and refrigerate. Toss and skewer bread cubes just before grilling.

SWEET CHILLI CHICKEN

SERVES 4

4 boneless, skinless chicken breasts
1 fresh red chilli, seeded and
 finely chopped
2 garlic cloves, crushed
1 tbsp grated fresh ginger
4 tbsp runny honey
2 tbsp soy sauce
4 tbsp lime juice

FOR GARNISHES

1 spring onion, diagonally sliced
1 fresh red chilli, seeded and
 finely sliced
1 tbsp fresh mint leaves
1 tbsp fresh coriander leaves

ESSENTIAL EQUIPMENT
4 - 35cm (14in) flat metal skewers

Cut each breast lengthwise into 3 strips. Combine chilli, garlic, ginger, honey, soy sauce and lime juice. Reserve 4 tbsp mixture. Add chicken to remaining mixture and toss to coat evenly. Cover and refrigerate for 30 minutes. Thread 3 chicken strips on to each skewer. Grill according to instructions below. Drizzle over reserved sweet chilli mixture. Sprinkle with spring onion, chilli, mint and coriander leaves. Serve hot.

OUTDOOR
Grill over medium-hot coals, turning every 2 minutes, until cooked through, 8-10 minutes.

INDOOR
Preheat overhead grill. Grill, turning every 2 minutes, until cooked through, 8-10 minutes.

THINK AHEAD
Marinate chicken up to 2 hours in advance. Cover and refrigerate.

COOKS' NOTE
This is Asian finger food. We also like to wrap up each succulent piece of chicken with its fragrant and spicy garnishes in a crisp, cool lettuce cup.

LEMON YOGHURT CHICKEN WRAP

SERVES 4

4 boneless, skinless chicken breasts
2 garlic cloves, crushed
¼ tsp ground cinnamon
¼ tsp ground allspice
1 tsp black pepper
1 tbsp olive oil
3 tbsp lemon juice
2 tbsp greek-style yoghurt

4 pitta or flatbreads
1 handful shredded iceberg
 or cos lettuce
4 tomatoes, sliced
8 radishes, sliced
salt
1 recipe roast garlic aïoli
 (see page 143)

ESSENTIAL EQUIPMENT
4 - 35cm (14in) flat metal skewers

Cut each breast lengthwise into 3 strips. Combine garlic, cinnamon, allspice, pepper, oil, lemon juice and yoghurt. Add chicken strips and toss to coat evenly. Cover and refrigerate for 30 minutes. Thread 3 chicken strips on to each skewer. Grill according to instructions below. Split open and separate each warmed pitta into 2 halves. Stack 2 pitta halves cut side up. Using a fork, slide the chicken pieces from 1 skewer on to the pitta. Top with a quarter of the lettuce, tomatoes and radishes. Spoon over aïoli. Add salt and pepper and roll up. Repeat with remaining pitta, chicken, lettuce, tomatoes, radishes and aïoli. Serve hot.

OUTDOOR
Grill over medium-hot coals, turning every 2 minutes, until cooked through, 8-10 minutes. Place pitta halves directly on the grill until just warm, about 30 seconds per side.

INDOOR
Preheat overhead grill. Grill, turning every 2 minutes, until cooked through, 8-10 minutes. Place pitta halves briefly under grill until warm, 15 seconds per side.

THINK AHEAD
Marinate chicken up to 3 hours in advance. Cover and refrigerate.

THAI SPICED CHICKEN WINGS

MAKES 20

2 lemon grass stalks
2 tbsp grated fresh ginger
5 garlic cloves, crushed
1 red onion, quartered
grated zest of 1 lime
2 tsp crushed chilli flakes
$\frac{1}{2}$ tsp ground coriander
$\frac{1}{2}$ tsp ground cumin

$\frac{1}{2}$ tsp paprika
2 tsp salt
1 tbsp sunflower oil
6 tbsp dark brown sugar
6 tbsp tomato purée
20 large chicken wings, tips cut off
  (see opposite)

ESSENTIAL EQUIPMENT
8 - 35cm (14in) flat metal skewers

Remove and discard the tough outer skin from the lemon grass stalks and roughly chop. Place lemon grass, ginger, garlic, onion, lime zest, chilli flakes, coriander, cumin, paprika, salt, oil, sugar and tomato purée in a food processor or blender; pulse until smooth. In a bowl, combine the mixture with the wings and toss to coat evenly. Cover and refrigerate for 2 hours. Thread the wings on to parallel skewers (see opposite). Grill according to instructions below. Serve hot.

OUTDOOR
Grill the wings over medium-hot coals for 20-25 minutes, turning every 5 minutes, until the meat at the bone is opaque.

INDOOR
Preheat grill. Arrange the wings on a wire rack over an oven tray. Grill for 15-20 minutes, turning once, until the meat at the bone is opaque.

THINK AHEAD
Marinate the wings up to 8 hours in advance. Make marinade up to 1 week in advance. Cover and refrigerate.

CUTTING OFF WING TIPS
To remove the wing tip, use a sharp pair of kitchen scissors and cut at the joint.

THREADING CHICKEN WINGS ON TO SKEWERS
Make sure that the skewers pass through the middle to secure both joints.

HONEY SOY CHICKEN WINGS

MAKES 20

6 tbsp dark soy sauce
3 tbsp dry sherry
2 tbsp runny honey
20 large chicken wings, tips cut off (see page 100)
1 recipe spicy peanut sauce (see page 136), optional

ESSENTIAL EQUIPMENT
8 - 35cm (14in) flat metal skewers

Combine soy sauce, sherry and honey in a bowl. Add the wings and toss to coat evenly. Cover and refrigerate for 2 hours. Thread the wings on to parallel skewers (see page 100). Grill according to instructions below. Serve hot with spicy peanut sauce, optional.

OUTDOOR
Grill over medium-hot coals for 20-25 minutes, turning every 5 minutes, until the meat at the bone is opaque.

INDOOR
Preheat grill. Arrange the wings on a wire rack over an oven tray. Grill for 15-20 minutes, turning once, until the meat at the bone is opaque.

THINK AHEAD
Marinate the wings up to 8 hours in advance. Cover and refrigerate.

SPICY LIME CHICKEN WINGS

MAKES 20

2 limes, peeled and chopped (see page 161)
2 garlic cloves, crushed
1 tsp chilli powder
1 tsp paprika
2 tsp granulated sugar
20 large chicken wings, tips cut off (see page 100)
2 tsp salt
1 recipe creamy avocado salsa (see page 132), optional

ESSENTIAL EQUIPMENT
8 - 35cm (14in) flat metal skewers

Combine lime flesh, garlic, chilli powder, paprika and sugar in a bowl. Add the wings and toss to coat evenly. Cover and refrigerate for 2 hours. Thread the wings on to parallel skewers (see page 100). Sprinkle evenly with salt. Serve hot with creamy avocado salsa for dipping, optional.

OUTDOOR
Grill wings over medium-hot coals for 20-25 minutes, turning every 5 minutes, until the meat at the bone is opaque.

INDOOR
Preheat grill. Arrange the wings on a wire rack over an oven tray. Grill for 15-20 minutes, turning once, until the meat at the bone is opaque.

THINK AHEAD
Marinate the wings up to 8 hours in advance. Cover and refrigerate.

SLASHING DRUMSTICKS
With sharp kitchen scissors, snip through skin to make deep cuts to the bone on both sides of the drumstick.

COOKS' NOTE
We slash drumsticks not only to allow flavouring to penetrate deeply, but to ensure that the meat is cooked through to the bone as quickly and evenly as possible.

HONEY MUSTARD CHICKEN DRUMSTICKS

SERVES 4

6 garlic cloves, crushed
3 tbsp runny honey
2 tbsp creamy dijon mustard
2 tbsp soy sauce
1 tbsp lemon juice

1 tsp black pepper
8 drumsticks, slashed (see opposite)
salt
1 recipe roast garlic aïoli (see page 143), optional

Combine garlic, honey, mustard, soy sauce, lemon juice and pepper. Add drumsticks and toss to coat evenly. Cover and refrigerate for 1 hour. Grill according to instructions below. Sprinkle with salt. Serve hot with roast garlic aïoli for dipping, optional.

OUTDOOR
Grill over medium hot coals, turning every 3 minutes, until the chicken is opaque with no trace of pink at the bone, 15 minutes.

INDOOR
Preheat overhead grill. Grill, turning every 3 minutes, until the chicken is opaque with no trace of pink at the bone, 15 minutes.

THINK AHEAD
Marinate drumsticks up to 6 hours in advance. Cover and refrigerate.

SPICY TANDOORI CHICKEN DRUMSTICKS

SERVES 4

juice of 1 lemon
2 tsp black pepper
8 chicken drumsticks, slashed
  (see page 102)
2 garlic cloves, crushed
1 tbsp grated fresh ginger
3 tbsp spicy tandoori mix
  (see page 25)
150ml (5floz) greek-style yoghurt
salt

Toss drumsticks with lemon juice and pepper. Cover and refrigerate for 30 minutes. Drain off lemon juice. Add garlic, ginger, tandoori mix and yoghurt to drumsticks. Toss to coat evenly. Cover and refrigerate for 1 hour. Shake off excess marinade and grill according to instructions below. Serve hot.

OUTDOOR
Grill over medium hot coals , turning every 3 minutes, until opaque with no trace of pink at the bone, 15 minutes.

INDOOR
Preheat overhead grill. Grill, turning every 3 minutes, until the chicken is opaque with no trace of pink at the bone,

THINK AHEAD
Marinate drumsticks up to 6 hours in advance. Cover and refrigerate.

LEMON GINGER CHICKEN DRUMSTICKS WITH MANGO AND MUSTARD SEED GLAZE

SERVES 4

8 chicken drumsticks, slashed
  (see page 102)

FOR MARINADE
2 tbsp grated fresh ginger
2 garlic cloves, crushed
½ tsp chilli powder
juice of 1 lemon

FOR GLAZE
4 tbsp mango chutney, sieved
1 tbsp yellow mustard seeds
salt

For marinade, combine ginger, garlic, chilli powder and lemon juice. Add drumsticks and toss to coat evenly. Cover and refrigerate for 30 minutes. For glaze, combine chutney and mustard seeds. Grill according to instructions below, brushing with glaze throughout. Sprinkle with salt. Serve hot.

OUTDOOR
Grill over medium hot coals , turning every 3 minutes, until the chicken is opaque with no trace of pink at the bone, 15 minutes.

INDOOR
Preheat overhead grill. Grill, turning every 3 minutes, until the chicken is opaque with no trace of pink at the bone, 15 minutes.

THINK AHEAD
Marinate drumsticks up to 4 hours in advance. Cover and refrigerate, turning several times in marinade.

BONING CHICKEN LEG

Place leg skin side down. With a small, sharp knife, cut down the thigh towards the leg joint to expose the thigh bone. Lift the bone, scraping and making small cuts to release the flesh from the bone.

Hold the released thigh bone, and cut around joint to free. With the tip of the knife scrape down the length of the drumstick bone to expose, scraping and pushing the meat down and away from you. Stop scraping when you get to the knuckle end, at which stage you will have turned the chicken leg inside out.

With large chef's knife, cut off the bone about 2.5cm (1in) from the knuckle end. Reshape the chicken leg by turning skin right side out again.

THINK AHEAD
Bone chicken leg up to 1 day in advance. Cover tightly with cling film and refrigerate.

CHICKEN LEGS STUFFED WITH WILD MUSHROOMS

SERVES 4
4 chicken legs, boned (see opposite)
2 tsp salt
1 tsp black pepper
FOR STUFFING
1 tbsp olive oil
2 garlic cloves, crushed
4 shallots, finely chopped
1 tbsp fresh thyme leaves
200g (7oz) fresh wild mushrooms (see below), chopped
dash of brandy
1 tsp white truffle oil, optional
salt, black pepper

extra olive oil for brushing
ESSENTIAL EQUIPMENT
4 - 25cm (10in) presoaked bamboo skewers

Sprinkle salt and pepper inside chicken legs.
Heat oil in frying pan over high heat until hot but not smoking. Add garlic, shallots, thyme and mushrooms. Stir fry until wilted and starting to crisp, 5 minutes. Add brandy. Stand back from pan and set alight with a long match. Allow flames to burn out, then remove pan from heat and leave to cool completely. Stir in truffle oil if using and add salt and pepper to taste. Place boned chicken legs skin side down. Using a tablespoon, push a quarter of the mushroom mixture inside each leg cavity. Use the back of the spoon to spread some of this mushroom mixture up on to the inside of the thigh. Wrap the thigh meat around the stuffing and reshape. Pull the skin over to seal and thread skewer through the thigh to secure flaps. Grill according to instructions below. Serve hot.

OUTDOOR
Grill over medium-hot coals, basting regularly, until meat is opaque and stuffing is cooked through, 7-10 minutes per side.

THINK AHEAD
Stuff chicken legs up to 6 hours in advance. Remove from refrigerator and bring to room temperature before placing on the grill.

COOKS' NOTE
Make sure that the mushroom mixture is completely cool before stuffing. Placing a hot mixture into uncooked chicken could present a health hazard when done in advance.

A bunch of herbs makes an aromatic alternative to a basting brush. Choose robust, woody herbs such as thyme or rosemary.

INDOOR
Preheat oven to 200°C (400°F) gas 6. Brush chicken with olive oil and place on oven tray. Roast until cooked through, 20-25 minutes.

WILD MUSHROOMS

There are many varieties of wild mushrooms. Field or shiitake mushrooms are excellent for this recipe. Field mushrooms have an open, flat cap with exposed brown gills and a strong, savoury flavour. Shiitake mushrooms are a widely available oriental variety with a powerful meaty flavour. For a deluxe selection, choose from a mixture of chanterelles, cèpes (also called porcini) and morels.

To clean mushrooms, wipe clean with damp kitchen paper. Never wash or rinse mushrooms in water.

TARRAGON MUSTARD CHICKEN SKEWERS

SERVES 4

8 boneless, skinless chicken
  thighs
2 tbsp dried tarragon
4 tbsp creamy dijon
  mustard
4 tbsp red wine vinegar
2 tsp paprika
1 tbsp granulated sugar
1 tsp black pepper
salt
1 recipe creamy blue
  cheese sauce (see page
  133), optional

ESSENTIAL EQUIPMENT
8 – 25cm (10 in) presoaked bamboo skewers

Cut each thigh into 6 equal-sized pieces. Thread pieces on to skewers. Combine tarragon, mustard, vinegar, paprika, sugar and pepper. Pour over skewered chicken. Cover and refrigerate for 30 minutes. Grill according to instructions below. Sprinkle with salt. Serve hot with creamy blue cheese sauce, optional.

OUTDOOR
Grill over medium-hot coals until the chicken is opaque with no trace of pink, 5 minutes per side.

INDOOR
Preheat overhead grill. Grill until the chicken is opaque with no trace of pink, 5 minutes per side.

THINK AHEAD
Marinate chicken up to 4 hours in advance. Cover and refrigerate.

CURRIED COCONUT CHICKEN

SERVES 4

8 boneless, skinless chicken
  thighs
4 garlic cloves, crushed
1 tbsp grated fresh ginger
1 onion, chopped
1 tbsp garam masala mix
  (see page 25)
1 handful fresh coriander
3 tbsp fish sauce
100ml (3½ floz) coconut
  milk
salt, black pepper
1 recipe oriental noodle
  salad (see page 150),
  optional

ESSENTIAL EQUIPMENT
16 – 25cm (10in) presoaked bamboo skewers

Spread chicken thighs flat. Thread 2 skewers diagonally through each thigh, to form a cross. Place garlic, ginger, onion, masala mix, coriander, fish sauce and coconut milk in a food processor or blender; pulse until smooth. Pour mixture over chicken. Cover and refrigerate for 30 minutes. Grill according to instructions below. Sprinkle with salt and pepper. Serve hot with oriental noodle salad, optional.

OUTDOOR
Grill over medium-hot coals until chicken is opaque with no trace of pink, 5 minutes per side.

INDOOR
Preheat overhead grill. Grill until chicken is opaque with no trace of pink, 5 minutes per side.

THINK AHEAD
Marinate chicken up to 6 hours in advance. Cover and refrigerate.

COOKS' NOTE
Skewering chicken thighs keeps them flat and open on the grill, allowing them to cook evenly.

GINGER HOISIN CHICKEN SKEWERS

SERVES 4

8 boneless, skinless chicken thighs
2 garlic cloves, chopped
3 tbsp grated fresh ginger
1 tbsp chinese hot chilli sauce

1 tbsp soy sauce
1 tbsp dark brown sugar
4 tbsp hoisin sauce
8 spring onions, trimmed

ESSENTIAL EQUIPMENT
8 - 25cm (10in) presoaked bamboo skewers

Cut thighs into 2.5cm (1in) cubes. Combine garlic, ginger, chilli sauce, soy sauce, sugar and hoisin. Add chicken and toss to coat evenly. Cover and refrigerate for 30 minutes. Divide chicken cubes equally and skewer. Thread a spring onion over either end of each skewer, to form a bow shape round the chicken pieces. Grill according to instructions below. Serve hot.

OUTDOOR
Grill over medium-hot coals until chicken is opaque with no trace of pink, 5 minutes per side.

INDOOR
Preheat overhead grill. Grill until chicken is opaque with no trace of pink, 5 minutes per side.

THINK AHEAD
Marinate chicken up to 4 hours in advance. Cover and refrigerate.

CARDAMOM CHICKEN TIKKA

SERVES 4

**8 boneless, skinless chicken thighs
juice of 1 lemon
2 tsp black pepper
1 tbsp grated fresh ginger
3 garlic cloves, crushed
1 tsp ground cardamom
½ tsp ground cumin
½ tsp ground nutmeg**

**1 fresh green chilli, seeded and
finely chopped
1 tbsp double cream
3 tbsp greek-style yoghurt
1½ lemons, cut into 8 wedges
salt
1 recipe cucumber yoghurt raita
(see page 138), optional**

ESSENTIAL EQUIPMENT
8 – 25cm (10in) presoaked bamboo skewers

Cut each thigh into 6 equal-sized pieces. Toss chicken pieces with lemon juice and pepper. Cover and refrigerate for 30 minutes. Drain off lemon juice. Add ginger, garlic, cardamom, cumin, nutmeg, chilli, cream and yoghurt to chicken. Toss together to coat chicken well. Cover and refrigerate for 1 hour. Remove chicken cubes from marinade, shaking off any excess. Thread on to skewers with lemon wedges. Grill according to instructions below. Sprinkle with salt. Serve hot with cucumber yoghurt raita, optional.

OUTDOOR
Grill over medium-hot coals until chicken is opaque with no trace of pink, 5 minutes per side.

INDOOR
Preheat overhead grill. Grill until the chicken is opaque with no trace of pink, 5 minutes per side.

THINK AHEAD
Marinate chicken up to 4 hours in advance. Cover and refrigerate.

COOKS' NOTE
It's best to grind the cardamom just before using, as its fragrance fades quickly after grinding. Lightly crush the pods to remove the grain-like seeds, then crush (see page 161) until finely ground.

TERIYAKI CHICKEN

SERVES 4

**4 tbsp shoyu (japanese soy sauce)
2 tbsp mirin
4 tbsp sake
1 tbsp granulated sugar
8 boneless, skinless chicken thighs**

ESSENTIAL EQUIPMENT
*8 attached pairs presoaked wooden chopsticks
or 8 - 25cm (10in) presoaked bamboo skewers*

Combine shoyu, mirin, sake and sugar in small pan over medium heat. Bring to the boil, stirring to dissolve the sugar. Lower heat and simmer until thick and syrupy, 5 -10 minutes. Cool. Set aside half the sauce for glazing the chicken. Reserve remaining half to drizzle over before serving. Cut each thigh into 3 even-sized pieces. Insert the blade of a small, sharp knife through the middle of each chicken piece to make a slit. Thread 3 slit pieces on to each pair of attached chopsticks. Brush all over with the cooled sauce to glaze. Grill according to instructions below, basting with sauce. Drizzle over reserved sauce. Serve hot.

OUTDOOR
Grill over medium hot coals until the chicken is opaque with no trace of pink, 7 minutes per side.

INDOOR
Preheat overhead grill. Grill until the chicken is opaque with no trace of pink, 7 minutes per side.

THINK AHEAD
Make sauce up to 3 days in advance. Cover and refrigerate.

COOKS' NOTE
We like to serve teriyaki chicken on pairs of chopsticks for a fun and impressive presentation. Since they do not have sharpened ends, use a knife to make an incision through the chicken to help you slide the chicken pieces onto the chopsticks. Alternatively, use presoaked bamboo skewers.

SPLITTING POULTRY

Place bird breast side down. With kitchen scissors or poultry shears, cut along each side of the backbone. Remove and discard.

Snip the wishbone and cut 1cm (½ in) into the breast bone so that the bird can be pressed flat

THINK AHEAD
Split bird up to 1 day in advance. Cover tightly with cling film and refrigerate.

COOKS' NOTE
Splitting is a useful technique for the grill. Opening the birds flat and making them an equal thickness allows for quick, even cooking. The meat is cooked throughout without drying out.

We prefer to start cooking split birds bone side down as the heat of the grill takes longer to penetrate the denser, bony side. You can turn your attention to colouring the skin side nicely once you are sure that the bird is on its way to being cooked through.

LEMON PEPPERED POUSSIN

SERVES 4

4 poussin, split (see opposite)
1 lemon, peeled and chopped
  (see page 161)
2 tsp crushed chilli flakes
2 garlic cloves, crushed

2 tbsp worcestershire sauce
4 tbsp sunflower oil
salt, black pepper
1 recipe roast garlic aïoli
  (see page 143), optional

ESSENTIAL EQUIPMENT
8 – 35cm (14in) flat metal skewers

Place a poussin cut side down and press flat. Push a skewer horizontally through the wings and breast. Push another skewer horizontally through the thighs. Repeat with remaining poussin and skewers.

Combine lemon, chilli flakes, garlic, worcestershire sauce and oil in a large dish. Add poussin, turning to coat both sides. Cover and refrigerate for 30 minutes. Grill according to instructions below. Remove skewers. Sprinkle with salt and pepper. Serve hot with roast garlic aïoli, optional.

OUTDOOR
Grill bone side down over medium-hot coals for 15 minutes. Turn and grill skin side down until skin is crispy and there is no trace of pink at the bone, 10 minutes.

INDOOR
Preheat overhead grill. Grill bone side up for 15 minutes. Turn and grill skin side up until skin is crispy and there is no trace of pink at the bone, 10 minutes.

THINK AHEAD
Marinate poussin up to 3 hours in advance. Cover and refrigerate, turning several times.

SPLIT POUSSIN VARIATION
SPICY JERK POUSSIN

Replace lemon, chilli flakes, garlic, worcestershire sauce and oil with spicy jerk rub (see page 24). Omit roast garlic aïoli when serving.

SCORING DUCK SKIN

With a sharp knife, cut diagonal parallel slashes 1cm (½in) apart through skin to make diamond pattern. Be careful not to pierce the flesh.

COOKS' NOTE
Scoring is essential if you want perfectly crisp duck. The scored surface allows the layer of fat under the skin to melt away so that the outer skin can crisp.

CRISPY BALSAMIC DUCK

SERVES 4
5 tbsp balsamic vinegar
4 duck breasts, scored (see opposite)
salt, black pepper
1 tbsp extra balsamic vinegar for drizzling

Put 5 tbsp vinegar in a shallow dish just wide enough to fit 4 breasts. Add the duck breasts, skin side up. Cover and leave to marinate for 20 minutes at room temperature. Grill or roast according to instructions below. Cover with foil and leave to rest for 5 minutes before cutting into thin slices (see below). Sprinkle with salt and pepper. Drizzle over remaining balsamic vinegar. Serve hot.

OUTDOOR
Grill over medium coals, skin side down until the skin is crispy, 5 minutes. Turn and grill for further 8 minutes for medium rare, 10 minutes for well-done.

INDOOR
Preheat oven to 200°C (400°F) gas 6. Preheat a heavy oven-proof pan over medium heat. Add duck skin side down and cook until crispy, 5 minutes. Turn breasts and place pan in the oven for 8 minutes for medium rare, 10 minutes for well done.

THINK AHEAD
Marinate duck breasts up to 2 hours in advance. Cover and refrigerate.

COOKS' NOTE
We like to serve this tangy duck dish with a slice of roasted onion focaccia with rosemary (see page 155).

SPICED SOY DUCK

SERVES 4
2 tbsp runny honey
1 tbsp soy sauce
½ tsp chinese five-spice powder
4 duck breasts, scored (see page 111)

Combine honey, soy sauce and spice. Put mixture in a shallow dish just wide enough to fit 4 breasts. Add the duck breasts, skin side up. Cover and leave to marinate for 20 minutes at room temperature. Grill or roast according to instructions below. Cover with foil and leave to rest for 5 minutes before slicing across on the diagonal. Serve hot.

OUTDOOR
Grill over medium coals, skin side down until the skin is crispy, 5 minutes. Turn and grill for a further 8 minutes for medium rare, 10 minutes for well done.

INDOOR
Preheat oven to 200°C (400°F) gas 6. Preheat a heavy oven-proof pan over medium heat. Add duck skin side down and cook until crispy, 5 minutes. Turn breasts and place pan in the oven for 8 minutes for medium rare, 10 minutes for well done.

THINK AHEAD
Marinate duck breasts up to 2 hours in advance. Cover and refrigerate.

COOKS' NOTE
Fresh papaya sambal (see page 137) and sesame soba noodle salad (see page 148) are both delicious accompaniments to this spicy duck.

DUCK WITH SWEET ORANGE GLAZE

SERVES 4

juice of 2 oranges
2 tbsp runny honey
4 duck breasts, scored (see page 111)
salt, black pepper

For glaze, combine 2 tbsp of the orange juice with honey. Put remaining orange juice in a shallow dish just wide enough for 4 breasts. Add the duck breasts, skin side up. Cover and leave to marinate for 20 minutes at room temperature. Grill or roast according to instructions below, basting with glaze throughout. Cover with foil and leave to rest for 5 minutes before cutting on the diagonal into thin slices. Sprinkle with salt and pepper. Serve hot.

OUTDOOR
Grill over medium coals, skin side down until the skin is crispy, 5 minutes. Turn and grill for further 8 minutes for medium rare, 10 minutes for well-done.

INDOOR
Preheat oven to 200°C (400°F) gas 6. Preheat a heavy oven-proof pan over medium heat. Add duck skin side down and cook until crispy, 5 minutes. Turn breasts and place pan in the oven for 8 minutes for medium rare, 10 minutes for well done.

THINK AHEAD
Marinate duck breasts up to 2 hours in advance. Cover and refrigerate.

COOKS' NOTE
A crisp, green leaf salad with honey mustard dressing (see page 152) is the perfect match for this succulent, savoury duck.

CINNAMON QUAIL WITH POMEGRANATE GLAZE

SERVES 4

8 quail, split (see page 110)
1 tsp ground cinnamon
2 tbsp pomegranate molasses
1 tbsp olive oil
salt, black pepper

ESSENTIAL EQUIPMENT
8 - 35cm (14in) flat metal skewers

Place 2 quail cut side down and press flat. Push a skewer horizontally through the wings and breast of both quail. Push another skewer horizontally through the thighs. Repeat with remaining quail and skewers. Combine cinnamon and pomegranate molasses and rub over quail. Cover with cling film and refrigerate for 30 minutes. Remove from refrigerator and bring to room temperature. Drizzle over oil. Grill according to instructions below. Sprinkle with salt and pepper. Serve hot.

OUTDOOR
Grill bone side down over medium-hot coals for 8 minutes. Turn and grill skin side down, until the meat is opaque and there is no trace of pink at the bone, a further 5 minutes.

INDOOR
Preheat overhead grill. Grill bone side up for 8 minutes. Turn and grill skin side up until skin is crispy and there is no trace of pink at the bone, a further 5 minutes.

THINK AHEAD
Marinate quail up to 4 hours in advance. Cover and refrigerate.

COOKS' NOTE
Pomegranate molasses - also referred to as syrup and concentrate - is made by boiling down pomegranate juice to a thick dark brown liquid with a distinctive sweet sour flavour. It's a favourite flavouring across the Middle East but especially in Iran, Syria and Lebanon. Look for it in Middle-Eastern shops or order it from a gourmet mail order company (see page 167). Alternatively, use date molasses, which is available in health food stores.

ROSEMARY GARLIC QUAIL

SERVES 4

8 quail, split (see page 110)
1 tsp dried rosemary
2 garlic cloves, crushed
½ tsp black pepper
¼ tsp crushed chilli flakes
1 tbsp lemon juice
1 tbsp olive oil

ESSENTIAL EQUIPMENT
8 - 35cm (14in) flat metal skewers

Place 2 quail cut side down and press flat. Push a skewer horizontally through the wings and breast of both quail. Push another skewer horizontally through the thighs. Repeat with remaining quail and skewers. Combine rosemary, garlic, pepper, chilli flakes, lemon juice and oil. Leave mixture to stand at room temperature for 30 minutes to allow flavours to combine. Brush mixture over quail. Grill according to instructions below, basting throughout with remaining mixture. Sprinkle with salt. Serve hot.

OUTDOOR
Grill bone side down over medium-hot coals for 8 minutes. Turn and grill skin side down, until the meat is opaque and there is no trace of pink at the bone, a further 5 minutes.

INDOOR
Preheat overhead grill. Grill bone side up for 8 minutes. Turn and grill skin side up until skin is crispy and there is no trace of pink at the bone, a further 5 minutes.

THINK AHEAD
Make marinade up to 1 day in advance. Cover and store at room temperature.

COOKS' NOTE
The intense, sun-filled flavours of slow roast tomato salad (see page 147) perfectly complement these grilled Tuscan-style quails. This aromatic and spciy marinade is also delicious with split poussin (see page 110 for cooking times).

VEGETABLES ON THE GRILL

CHARGRILLED BALSAMIC RED ONIONS

SERVES 4
2 large red onions
2 tbsp olive oil
1 tbsp balsamic vinegar
salt, black pepper
1 tbsp each extra olive oil and balsamic vinegar to drizzle
1 tsp fresh thyme leaves

ESSENTIAL EQUIPMENT
4 – 35cm (14in) flat metal skewers

Trim off and discard the root and stalk ends of the onions. Cut each onion into 1.5cm (¾in) rounds. Thread rounds on to skewers. Brush both sides of each skewered round with oil. Sprinkle with balsamic vinegar, salt and pepper. Grill according to instructions below. Drizzle over remaining oil and vinegar. Sprinkle with thyme. Serve hot.

OUTDOOR
Grill over medium coals until tender and lightly charred, 5 minutes per side.

INDOOR
Preheat overhead grill. Grill until lightly charred, 5 minutes per side.

CHAR-ROAST ROSEMARY ONIONS

SERVES 4
4 unpeeled large yellow or red onions
2 tbsp red wine or sherry vinegar
2 tbsp olive oil
salt, black pepper
1 tsp finely chopped fresh rosemary
2 tbsp olive oil to drizzle
½ tbsp fresh rosemary leaves

Preheat oven to 180°C (350°F) gas 4.
Cut onions in half from top to bottom. Trim and peel each onion half, leaving the root end attached to allow the onion halves to stay intact when cooking. Arrange onion halves on an oven tray, cut side up. Sprinkle evenly with vinegar, oil, salt, pepper and chopped rosemary. Cover with foil and pre-roast for 30 minutes. Grill according to instructions below. Drizzle with olive oil and sprinkle with rosemary leaves. Serve hot.

OUTDOOR
Grill over medium-hot coals until lightly charred, 5 minutes per side.

INDOOR
Preheat overhead grill. Grill until lightly charred, 5 minutes per side.

THINK AHEAD
Pre-roast onions in oven up to 1 day in advance. Cover and store at room temperature.

COOKS' NOTE
These onions make a great vegetarian main course when served with creamy blue cheese sauce (see page 133).

CHARGRILLED CORN ON THE COB WITH CORIANDER CHILLI BUTTER

SERVES 4
4 ears fresh sweetcorn
2 tbsp melted butter
salt, black pepper
4 - 1.5cm (¾ in) slices coriander chilli butter
  (see page 140)
lime wedges

Cook corn in unsalted boiling water for 2 minutes. Refresh in cold water. Brush with melted butter. Grill according to instructions below. Sprinkle with salt and pepper. Serve each ear hot with a slice of coriander chilli butter and a wedge of lime.

OUTDOOR
Grill over medium-hot coals, turning frequently, until lightly charred, 5 minutes.

INDOOR
Preheat overhead grill. Grill, turning frequently until lightly charred, 5 minutes.

THINK AHEAD
Boil corn up to 1 day in advance. Refresh immediately in cold water. Cover and refrigerate. Grill just before serving.

COOKS' NOTE
We also love chargrilled corn on the cob spread with roast garlic aïoli (see page 143).

CHAR-ROAST PEPPERS

SERVES 4
3 red, yellow or orange peppers
1 tbsp balsamic vinegar
3 tbsp olive oil
salt, black pepper

Grill peppers whole according to instructions below. Place grilled peppers in a plastic bag or a bowl with a plate on top. Leave for 5-10 minutes until cool enough to handle. Uncover and peel off charred skin. Discard stems and seeds (see page 160). Slice peppers into 1cm (½ in) wide strips. Toss strips with vinegar and oil. Add salt and pepper to taste. Serve warm or at room temperature.

OUTDOOR
Grill over flaming coals, turning frequently, until skin is charred all over, 10 minutes.

INDOOR
Preheat overhead grill. Place under grill, turning frequently, until skin is charred all over, 10 minutes.

THINK AHEAD
Grill peppers up to 1 day in advance. Store covered at room temperature.

CHARGRILLED NEW POTATO SKEWERS

SERVES 4

750g (1½ lb) unpeeled new potatoes
3 tbsp olive oil
salt, black pepper

ESSENTIAL EQUIPMENT
4 - 25cm (10in) presoaked bamboo skewers

Cook potatoes in boiling salted water until just tender, 15 minutes. Cut in half and toss with oil, salt and pepper. Thread potato halves on to skewers. Grill according to instructions below. Serve hot.

OUTDOOR
Grill over medium coals, turning regularly, until lightly charred, 10 minutes.

INDOOR
Preheat overhead grill. Grill, turning regularly, until lightly charred, 10 minutes.

THINK AHEAD
Pre-cook potatoes up to 1 day in advance. Cut in half, toss in oil and skewer up to 2 hours in advance. Cover and keep at room temperature until ready to grill.

CHARGRILLED TOMATOES

SERVES 4

4 ripe tomatoes, halved
1 tbsp olive oil
salt, black pepper

Place tomato halves skin side down. Sprinkle with oil, salt and pepper. Grill according to instructions below. Serve hot or at room temperature.

OUTDOOR
Grill over medium-hot coals until lightly charred on the outside but still firm, 3 minutes per side.

INDOOR
Preheat overhead grill. Grill until lightly charred on the outside but still firm, 3 minutes per side.

CHARGRILLED GARLIC POTATO SLICES

SERVES 4

750g (1½ lb) unpeeled plain or sweet potatoes, sliced
1cm (½ in) thick
2 garlic cloves, crushed
4 tbsp olive oil
salt, black pepper
1 recipe roast garlic aïoli (see page 143), optional

Cook potato slices in boiling salted water until tender but still firm, 5 minutes. Drain. Combine the garlic and oil. Brush potato slices with garlic oil. Grill according to instructions below. Sprinkle with salt and pepper. Serve hot with aïoli, optional.

OUTDOOR
Grill over medium coals until lightly charred, 5 minutes per side.

INDOOR
Preheat overhead grill. Grill until lightly charred, 5 minutes per side.

THINK AHEAD
Boil potato slices up to 4 hours in advance. Cool, cover and keep at room temperature until ready to grill.

CHARGRILLED AUBERGINE SLICES WITH LEMON TAHINI SAUCE

SERVES 4

2 aubergines cut into 1cm (½ in) thick slices
8 tbsp olive oil
salt, black pepper
1 recipe lemon tahini sauce (see page 132)

Brush the aubergine slices on both sides with olive oil. Grill according to instructions below. Sprinkle with salt and pepper. Serve hot or at room temperature with lemon tahini sauce.

OUTDOOR
Grill over medium-hot coals until lightly charred and tender, 5 minutes per side.

INDOOR
Preheat a ridged cast iron grill pan over high heat. Grill until lightly charred and tender, 5 minutes per side.

THINK AHEAD
Grill aubergines up to 6 hours in advance. Cover and store at room temperature.

COOKS' NOTE
Salsa verde (see page 134), charmoula (see page 23), spicy peanut sauce (see page 136), roast pepper and basil salsa (see page 138) or spiced chickpea sauce (see page 137) are all excellent choices to serve with these aubergine slices in place of the lemon tahini sauce.

CHAR-ROAST AUBERGINE WITH SESAME AND HONEY MISO GLAZE

SERVES 4

4 tbsp honey miso sauce (see page 138)
2 tbsp sesame seeds
2 aubergines
extra honey miso sauce for drizzling

For glaze, combine honey miso sauce and sesame seeds. Prick aubergines all over with fork. Grill according to instructions below. Cut in half lengthwise. Score a crisscross pattern 1cm (½ in) deep into the aubergine flesh. Brush scored side with glaze. Grill glazed cut side down until sizzling and tender, a further 5 minutes. Serve hot with extra honey miso sauce drizzled over.

OUTDOOR
Grill over medium coals, turning frequently until charred all over, 15 minutes. Leave until cool enough to handle, about 10 minutes.

INDOOR
Preheat overhead grill. Grill, turning frequently, until charred all over, 15 minutes. Leave until cool enough to handle, about 10 minutes.

AUBERGINE VARIATION

CHAR-ROAST AUBERGINE WITH SPICY PEANUT SAUCE

SERVES 4

Omit honey miso sauce and sesame seeds. Spread scored side of aubergines with 4 tbsp spicy peanut sauce (see page 136). Serve with remaining spicy peanut sauce.

CHARGRILLED COURGETTES WITH ROAST PEPPER AND BASIL SALSA

SERVES 4

500g (1lb) courgettes, sliced 1cm (½in) thick lengthwise
3 tbsp olive oil
salt, black pepper
1 recipe roast pepper and basil salsa (see page 138)

Grill courgettes according to instructions below. Arrange on platter. Spoon over salsa and serve hot or at room temperature.

OUTDOOR
Grill over medium coals until lightly charred and tender, 5 -10 minutes per side.

INDOOR
Preheat a ridged cast iron grill pan over high heat. Grill until lightly charred and tender, 5-10 minutes per side.

COOKS' NOTE
This makes a great vegetarian main course when served with radish tzatziki (see page 135) or creamy blue cheese sauce (see page 133).

CHARGRILLED SQUASH WITH JERKED HONEY RUM GLAZE

SERVES 4

500g (1lb) unpeeled butternut squash, cut into
   1cm (½in) thick slices
1 recipe jerked honey rum glaze (see page 25)
salt, black pepper

Bring a large pan of water to the boil. Add squash slices and when water returns to rolling boil, drain. Arrange in a single layer on a tea towel and pat dry. Grill according to instructions below. Sprinkle with salt and pepper and serve hot.

OUTDOOR
Grill over medium-hot coals, brushing with glaze and turning once until lightly charred, 3 minutes per side.

INDOOR
Preheat overhead grill. Brush with glaze and grill until browned, 3 minutes per side.

THINK AHEAD
Pre-cook squash up to 4 hours in advance. Cover and leave at room temperature until ready to grill.

CHARGRILLED NECTARINES

SERVES 4

4 nectarines, halved and stoned
1 tbsp runny honey
vanilla ice cream

Brush cut sides of nectarine halves with honey. Grill according to instructions below. Serve hot with a scoop of vanilla ice cream.

OUTDOOR
Grill cut side down over medium-low coals until warm and lightly charred, but still firm, 5 minutes.

INDOOR
Preheat overhead grill. Grill cut side up until warm and lightly charred, but still firm, 5 minutes.

CHARGRILLED PINEAPPLE WITH SWEET RUM GLAZE

SERVES 4

1 unpeeled medium pineapple, quartered
2 tbsp dark rum
1 tbsp lime juice
2 tbsp honey

Cut away the core from the pineapple quarters. For glaze, combine rum, lime juice and honey and stir to dissolve. Grill according to instructions below. Serve hot with any remaining glaze drizzled over.

OUTDOOR
Grill over medium-low coals, brushing with glaze, until hot and lightly charred, 5 -10 minutes per side.

INDOOR
Preheat overhead grill. Brush with glaze and grill until hot and lightly charred, 5 -10 minutes per side.

VARIATION

CHARGRILLED PINEAPPLE WITH JERKED HONEY RUM GLAZE

Replace sweet rum glaze with jerked honey rum glaze (see page 25).

GRILL ROAST CINNAMON RUM BANANAS

SERVES 4

**4 large bananas, cut on diagonal into
  2.5cm (1in) thick slices
juice of 1 lime
1 tbsp dark brown sugar
2 tbsp dark rum
1 tsp ground cinnamon
vanilla ice cream**

ESSENTIAL EQUIPMENT
4 - 30cm (12in) squares of extra thick or heavy duty foil

Toss banana slices with lime juice, sugar, rum and cinnamon. Divide bananas among foil squares. Bring the edges of foil together and scrunch to seal. Grill roast according to instructions below. Serve warm with a scoop of vanilla ice cream.

OUTDOOR
Grill over medium-low coals until hot through, 15-20 minutes.

INDOOR
Preheat oven to 200°C (400°F) gas 6. Bake until hot through, 10-15 minutes.

THINK AHEAD
Assemble foil packets up to 1 hour in advance. Store at room temperature.

GRILL ROAST LEMON LIQUEUR STRAWBERRIES

SERVES 4

**500g (1lb) strawberries, hulled and halved
3 tbsp grand marnier
grated zest of 1 lemon
2 tbsp granulated sugar
vanilla ice cream**

ESSENTIAL EQUIPMENT
4 - 30cm (12in) squares of extra thick or heavy duty foil

Toss strawberry halves with grand marnier, lemon zest and sugar. Divide strawberries among foil squares. Bring the edges of foil together and scrunch to seal. Grill roast according to instructions below. Serve warm with a scoop of vanilla ice cream.

OUTDOOR
Grill over medium-low coals until warm through, 5-10 minutes.

INDOOR
Preheat oven to 200°C (400°F) gas 6. Bake until warm through, 5 minutes.

THINK AHEAD
Assemble foil packets up to 1 hour in advance. Store at room temperature.

GRILL ROAST SWEET SPICED ORANGES

SERVES 4

**4 oranges, peeled (see page 161) and cut into
  2.5cm (1in) slices
1½ tbsp dark brown sugar
2 tsp brandy
1 tsp cardamom pods**

ESSENTIAL EQUIPMENT
4 - 30cm (12in) squares of extra thick or heavy duty foil

Toss orange slices with sugar and brandy. Divide orange slices among foil squares. Sprinkle with cardamom pods. Bring the edges of foil together and scrunch to seal. Grill roast according to instructions below. Serve hot.

OUTDOOR
Grill over medium-low coals until hot through, 15-20 minutes.

INDOOR
Preheat oven to 200°C (400°F) gas 6. Bake until hot through, 10-15 minutes.

THINK AHEAD
Assemble foil packets up to 2 hours in advance. Store at room temperature.

GRILL ROAST HONEY ORANGE FIGS

SERVES 4

**8 figs, halved
4 tbsp runny honey
juice of 1 orange
grated zest of 1 orange
4 tbsp mascarpone or crème fraîche**

ESSENTIAL EQUIPMENT
4 - 30cm (12in) squares of extra thick or heavy duty foil

Divide fig halves cut side up among foil squares. Drizzle over honey and orange juice and sprinkle with zest. Bring the edges of foil together and scrunch to seal. Grill roast according to instructions below. Serve hot with mascarpone or crème fraîche.

OUTDOOR
Grill over medium-low coals until hot through, 15-20 minutes.

INDOOR
Preheat oven to 200°C (400°F) gas 6. Bake until hot through, 10-15 minutes.

THINK AHEAD
Assemble foil packets up to 2 hours in advance. Store at room temperature.

CHARGRILLED QUESADILLAS WITH SALSA FRESCA

SERVES 4

8 - 20cm (8in) flour tortillas
100g (3½oz) gruyère cheese, grated
1 recipe salsa fresca (see page 133)
200g (7oz) feta cheese, crumbled
1 recipe creamy avocado salsa (see page 132), optional

Spread a quarter of the gruyère over 1 tortilla. Top evenly
with a quarter of the salsa fresca. Sprinkle with a quarter of
the feta. Lightly press a second tortilla on top. Repeat with
remaining tortillas, gruyère, salsa and feta. Grill according to
instructions below. Cut into wedges with kitchen scissors or a
sharp serrated knife. Serve hot with creamy avocado salsa
spooned over each wedge, if desired.

OUTDOOR
Grill over medium-hot coals until lightly
charred and the gruyère is melted,
2 minutes per side.

INDOOR
Preheat a ridged cast iron grill pan over
high heat. Grill until lightly charred and
the gruyère is melted, 2 minutes
per side.

THINK AHEAD
Assemble tortillas up to 4 hours in advance. Cover with cling film and leave at room
temperature until ready to grill.

CHARGRILLED QUESADILLAS WITH SPICY CORIANDER

SERVES 4

1 handful fresh coriander
2 garlic cloves, crushed
1 green chilli, seeded and finely chopped
4 spring onions, chopped
½ tsp ground coriander
½ tsp ground cumin
2 tbsp lime juice
8 tbsp olive oil
salt, black pepper
8 - 20cm (8in) flour tortillas
200g (7oz) gruyère cheese, grated
1 recipe avocado mango salsa (see page 136)
150ml (5floz) sour cream, optional

Place fresh coriander, garlic, chilli, spring onion, ground
coriander, cumin, lime juice and oil in a food processor or
blender; pulse to a smooth paste. Add salt and pepper to taste.
Spread a quarter of the coriander paste over 1 tortilla. Top
evenly with a quarter of the cheese. Lightly press a second tortilla on top. Repeat with remaining tortillas, salsa and cheese.
Grill according to instructions below. Cut into wedges with
kitchen scissors or a sharp serrated knife. Serve hot with
avocado mango salsa and sour cream, optional, spooned over
each wedge.

OUTDOOR
Grill over medium-hot coals until
lightly charred and the cheese is
melted, 2 minutes per side.

INDOOR
Preheat a ridged cast iron grill pan
over high heat. Grill until lightly
charred and the cheese is melted,
2 minutes per side.

THINK AHEAD
Assemble tortillas up to 4 hours in advance. Cover with cling film and leave at room
temperature until ready to grill.

CHARGRILLED AUBERGINE, GOAT'S CHEESE AND MINT BRUSCHETTA

SERVES 4

8 slices day old ciabatta or country-style bread, 1cm (½ in) thick
1 medium aubergine, cut crosswise into 1cm (½ in) thick slices
4 tbsp olive oil for brushing

FOR DRESSING

1 tbsp finely chopped fresh mint
1 tbsp balsamic vinegar
1 tbsp olive oil
salt, black pepper

8 tbsp fresh creamy goat's cheese
extra olive oil for drizzling

Toast bread slices until crisp, about 2 minutes per side.

Brush the aubergine slices on both sides with olive oil. Grill according to instructions below. Toss aubergine slices gently with mint, vinegar and oil. Sprinkle with salt and pepper to taste.

Spread bruschetta with equal amounts of goat's cheese. Top with aubergine and drizzle with extra olive oil. Serve at room temperature.

OUTDOOR
Grill over medium-hot coals until lightly charred and tender, 5 minutes per side.

INDOOR
Preheat a ridged cast iron grill pan over high heat. Grill until lightly charred and tender, 5 minutes per side.

THINK AHEAD
Toast bruschetta up to 1 day in advance. Store in an airtight container at room temperature. Grill aubergine up to 6 hours in advance. Leave covered at room temperature until ready to serve.

CHAR-ROAST LEMON OREGANO PEPPERS ON BRUSCHETTA

SERVES 4

8 slices of day old ciabatta or country-style bread, 1cm (½ in) thick
3 red peppers
2 tbsp lemon juice

2 garlic cloves, crushed
2 tsp finely chopped fresh oregano
5 tbsp olive oil
salt, black pepper

Toast bread slices until crisp, 2 minutes per side.

Grill peppers according to instructions below. Place grilled peppers in a plastic bag or a bowl with a plate on top. Leave for 5-10 minutes until cool enough to handle. Uncover and peel off charred skin (see page 160). Discard stems and seeds (see page 160). Slice peppers into 1cm (½ in) wide strips. Toss strips with lemon, garlic, oregano and oil. Add salt and pepper to taste. Top bruschetta with equal amounts of dressed peppers. Serve warm or at room temperature.

OUTDOOR
Grill over flaming coals, turning frequently, until skin is charred all over, 10 minutes.

INDOOR
Preheat overhead grill. Place under grill, turning frequently, until skin is charred all over, 10 minutes.

THINK AHEAD
Prepare bruschetta and peppers up to one day in advance. Store bruschetta in an airtight container at room temperature. Store peppers separately at room temperature.

Sauces & Salsas

CREAMY AVOCADO SALSA

MAKES 500ml (16floz)
2 avocados, halved and stoned
6 spring onions, chopped
1 handful fresh coriander
2 tbsp red wine vinegar
2 tbsp olive oil
250ml (8floz) sour cream
salt, black pepper

Place avocado, spring onion, coriander, vinegar, oil and sour cream in a food processor or blender; pulse to a smooth purée. Add salt and pepper to taste. Cover and refrigerate for 30 minutes to allow flavours to blend. Serve chilled.

THINK AHEAD
Make salsa up to 1 day in advance. Cover and refrigerate.

COOKS' NOTE
To prevent discoloration, store in a bowl with cling film, pressing directly on the salsa to prevent contact with air.

LEMON TAHINI SAUCE

MAKES 250ml (8floz)
100ml (3½ floz) tahini
1 garlic clove, crushed
juice of 1 lemon
125ml (4floz) water
salt, black pepper

Whisk tahini, garlic and lemon juice together until smooth. Whisk in water. Add salt and pepper to taste. Cover and let stand at room temperature for 30 minutes to allow flavours to blend. Serve chilled or at room temperature.

THINK AHEAD
Make sauce up to 2 days in advance. Cover and refrigerate.

CREAMY BLUE CHEESE SAUCE

MAKES 500ml (16floz)
6 spring onions, chopped
200g (7oz) blue cheese
300ml (10floz) sour cream
1 tsp worcestershire sauce
salt, black pepper

Place spring onion, cheese, cream and worcestershire sauce in a food processor or blender; pulse until smooth. Add salt and pepper to taste. Cover and refrigerate for 30 minutes to allow flavours to blend. Serve chilled.

THINK AHEAD
Make sauce up to 1 day in advance. Cover and refrigerate. Leave to stand at room temperature for 15 minutes to soften slightly before serving.

SALSA FRESCA

MAKES ABOUT 375ml (13floz)
6 medium tomatoes, seeded (see page 161)
  and finely diced
1 red onion, finely chopped
2 garlic cloves, crushed
1 fresh green chilli, seeded and finely chopped
1 tbsp lime juice
2 tbsp olive oil
2 tbsp finely chopped fresh coriander
salt, black pepper

Combine tomatoes, onion, garlic, chilli, lime juice, oil and coriander. Add salt and pepper to taste. Cover and let stand for 30 minutes at room temperature to allow flavours to blend. Serve chilled or at room temperature.

THINK AHEAD
Make salsa up to 1 day in advance. Cover and refrigerate.

SALSA VERDE

MAKES 175ml (6floz)
2 handfuls flat-leaf parsley
10 fresh basil leaves
10 fresh mint leaves
1 garlic clove, crushed
1 tbsp creamy dijon mustard
1 tbsp drained capers
2 anchovy fillets
½ tsp red wine vinegar
150ml (5floz) olive oil
salt, black pepper

Place parsley, basil, mint, garlic, mustard, capers, anchovy, vinegar and oil in a food processor or blender; pulse to a purée. Add salt and pepper to taste. Cover and let stand for 30 minutes at room temperature to allow flavours to blend. Serve at room temperature.

THINK AHEAD
Make salsa up to 3 days in advance. Cover and refrigerate. Bring to room temperature and stir before serving.

PINEAPPLE LIME SALSA

MAKES 375ml (13floz)
½ fresh pineapple, cored
 and finely diced
1 fresh red chilli, seeded
 and finely chopped
1 red onion, finely chopped
2 tbsp finely chopped fresh
 coriander or mint
grated zest 1 lime
3 tbsp lime juice
salt, tabasco

Combine pineapple, chilli, onion, coriander or mint, lime zest and lime juice. Add salt and tabasco to taste. Cover and let stand for 30 minutes at room temperature to allow flavours to blend. Serve chilled or at room temperature.

THINK AHEAD
Make salsa up to 3 hours in advance. Cover and refrigerate.

COOKS' NOTE
A serrated knife is the best tool for cutting away the peel from a fresh pineapple. Cut off the leaves at their base and the bottom rind first. Stand the pineapple on its base and cut off the rind from the sides, using downward strokes.

RADISH TZATZIKI

MAKES 500ml (16floz)

150g (5oz) radishes, grated
1 red onion, grated
2 garlic cloves, crushed
1 tbsp red wine vinegar
1 tsp granulated sugar
175ml (6floz) greek-style yoghurt
salt, black pepper

Combine radishes, onion, garlic, vinegar, sugar and yoghurt. Add salt and pepper to taste. Cover and refrigerate for 30 minutes to allow flavours to blend. Serve chilled.

THINK AHEAD
Make tzatziki up to 1 day in advance. Cover and refrigerate. Stir before serving.

CHIMI CHURRI

MAKES 175ml (6floz)

2 handfuls flat-leaf parsley leaves
4 spring onions, chopped
8 garlic cloves, crushed
1 tsp dried oregano
½ tsp crushed chilli flakes
4 tbsp red wine vinegar
8 tbsp sunflower oil
salt, black pepper

Place parsley, spring onion, garlic, oregano, chilli flakes, vinegar and oil in a food processor or blender; pulse until well blended but still retaining some texture. Add salt and pepper to taste. Cover and let stand for 30 minutes at room temperature to allow flavours to blend. Serve chilled or at room temperature.

THINK AHEAD
Make up to 3 days in advance, but add the vinegar just 2 hours before serving.

COOKS' NOTE
When making this colourful sauce more than a couple of hours in advance, be sure to follow the instructions for adding vinegar at a later time. If added too far in advance, the vinegar will "cook" the parsley, causing the vibrant green colour of the sauce to fade.

AVOCADO MANGO SALSA

MAKES 375ml (13floz)

1 mango, finely diced
1 avocado, halved, stoned and finely diced
½ red onion, finely chopped
1 red chilli, seeded and finely chopped
1 tbsp lime juice
1 tbsp red wine vinegar
2 tbsp olive oil
2 tbsp finely chopped mint
salt, tabasco

Combine mango, avocado, onion, chilli, lime juice, vinegar, oil and mint. Add salt and tabasco to taste. Cover and let stand for 30 minutes at room temperature to allow flavours to blend. Serve chilled or at room temperature.

THINK AHEAD
Make salsa up to 6 hours before serving. Cover and refrigerate.

COOKS' NOTE
To prevent discoloration, store in a bowl with cling film, pressing directly on the salsa to prevent contact with air.

SPICY PEANUT SAUCE

MAKES 500ml (16floz)

250g (8oz) peanut butter
2 garlic cloves, crushed
1 tbsp grated fresh ginger
1 tsp turmeric
1 tsp tabasco
1 tbsp toasted sesame oil
4 tbsp soy sauce
2 tbsp runny honey
juice of 1 lemon
125ml (4floz) water

Place peanut butter, garlic, ginger, turmeric, tabasco, oil, soy sauce, honey, lemon juice and water in a food processor or blender; pulse until smooth. Cover and let stand for 30 minutes at room temperature to allow flavours to blend. Serve chilled or at room temperature.

THINK AHEAD
Make sauce up to 3 days in advance. Cover and refrigerate.

COOKS' NOTE
For a spicy peanut dip with an extra rich coconut flavour, replace the water with an equal amount of coconut milk.

FRESH PAPAYA SAMBAL

MAKES ABOUT 250ml (8floz)

1 papaya, seeded and finely chopped
½ red onion, finely chopped
1 tbsp finely chopped coriander
2 tbsp lime juice
1 tbsp fish sauce
1 tsp sugar
salt, black pepper

Combine papaya, onion, coriander, lime juice, fish sauce and sugar. Add salt and pepper to taste. Cover and let stand for 30 minutes at room temperature to allow flavours to blend. Serve chilled or at room temperature.

THINK AHEAD
Make sambal up to 4 hours in advance. Cover and refrigerate. Stir before serving.

COOKS' NOTE
This recipe is also delicious when mango is used in place of the papaya.

SPICED CHICKPEA SAUCE

MAKES 500ml (16floz)

1 - 400g (14oz) tin chickpeas, drained and rinsed
2 garlic cloves, crushed
½ tsp ground cumin
¼ tsp tabasco
2 tbsp lemon juice
5 tbsp tahini
5 tbsp water
125ml (4floz) greek-style yoghurt
salt, black pepper

Place chickpeas, garlic, cumin, tabasco, lemon juice, tahini, water and yoghurt in a food processor or blender; pulse until smooth. Add salt and pepper to taste. Cover and refrigerate for 30 minutes to allow flavours to blend. Serve chilled.

THINK AHEAD
Make sauce up to 3 days in advance. Cover and refrigerate.

137

HONEY MISO SAUCE

MAKES 125ml (4floz)

4 tbsp miso (see page 159)
4 tbsp runny honey
1 tbsp creamy dijon mustard
2 tbsp grated fresh ginger
2 garlic cloves, crushed
1½ tbsp soy sauce
1½ tbsp cider vinegar

Whisk miso, honey, mustard, ginger, garlic, soy sauce and vinegar together until smooth. Cover and let stand for 30 minutes at room temperature to allow flavours to blend. Serve at room temperature.

THINK AHEAD
Make sauce up to 1 day in advance. Cover and store at room temperature.

CUCUMBER YOGHURT RAITA

MAKES 500ml (16floz)

1 unpeeled cucumber, seeded and grated
2 spring onions, finely chopped
1 garlic clove, crushed
½ tbsp grated fresh ginger
2 tbsp finely chopped fresh mint
3 tbsp lemon juice
375ml (13floz) greek-style yoghurt
salt, black pepper
1 tsp cumin seeds, toasted

Combine cucumber, spring onion, garlic, ginger, mint, lemon juice and yoghurt. Add salt and pepper to taste. Cover and refrigerate for 30 minutes to allow flavours to blend. Sprinkle over cumin seeds. Serve chilled.

THINK AHEAD
Make raita up to 1 day in advance. Cover and refrigerate. Stir before serving.

CORIANDER COCONUT SAUCE

MAKES 500ml (16floz)

1 handful fresh coriander leaves
1 handful fresh mint leaves
4 garlic cloves, crushed
1 green chilli, seeded and chopped
1 avocado, halved and stoned
½ tsp ground cumin
1 tsp sugar
3 tbsp lime juice
200ml (7floz) coconut milk
salt, tabasco

Place coriander, mint, garlic, chilli, avocado, cumin, sugar, lime juice and coconut milk in a food processor or blender; pulse to a purée. Add salt and tabasco to taste. Cover and refrigerate for 30 minutes to allow flavours to blend. Serve chilled.

THINK AHEAD
Make sauce up to 1 day in advance. Cover and refrigerate. Stir before serving.

COOKS' NOTE
To prevent discoloration, store in a bowl with cling film, pressing directly on the sauce to prevent contact with air.

ROAST PEPPER AND BASIL SALSA

MAKES 250ml (8floz)

3 red peppers
2 garlic cloves, finely chopped
10 fresh basil leaves, torn
1 tbsp red wine vinegar
3 tbsp olive oil
salt, black pepper

Grill, peel and seed the peppers (see page 160). Cut into fine dice. Combine peppers, garlic, basil, vinegar and oil. Add salt and pepper to taste. Cover and let stand for 30 minutes at room temperature to allow flavours to blend.

THINK AHEAD
Make salsa up to 1 day in advance but add basil not more than 2 hours before serving. Cover and refrigerate. Bring back to room temperature and stir before serving.

MAKING FLAVOURED BUTTERS
Cut a piece of foil, approximately 25cm x 20cm (10in x 8in). Spread the butter in a block about 15cm (6in) long and 5cm (2in) thick in the middle of the foil. Roll up.

Twist the ends tightly to form an evenly shaped cylinder.

COOKS' NOTE
Flavoured butters are practical and easy. They can be made well in advance, frozen and sliced to order. Place a cold slice of flavoured butter on any food hot off the grill to create a simple, flavourful sauce with minimal effort.

CORIANDER CHILLI BUTTER

MAKES 15 SERVINGS

250g (8oz) unsalted butter, softened	1 tbsp lime juice
1 handful fresh coriander, chopped	2 tsp salt
1 fresh red chilli, seeded and chopped	1 tsp black pepper

Place ingredients in a food processor or blender; pulse until well blended. Wrap in foil (see opposite). Place in the freezer until hard, about 45 minutes. To serve, roll back foil and cut into 1cm (½in) slices. When slicing from frozen, warm the knife through under hot water first. After slicing, always tightly re-wrap the unused flavoured butter roll in the foil before returning to refrigerator or freezer.

THINK AHEAD
Make up to 6 weeks in advance and refrigerate. Alternatively, make up to 9 months in advance and place in freezer. To keep sliced butter chilled outdoors, float slices in a bowl of cold water and ice.

VARIATION
GARLIC PARSLEY BUTTER

MAKES 15 SERVINGS

Replace fresh coriander with the same amount of flat-leaf parsley. Replace lime juice with the same amount of lemon juice. Replace red chilli with 5 crushed garlic cloves.

BLUE CHEESE BUTTER

MAKES 15 SERVINGS

250g (8oz) unsalted butter, softened	2 tsp black pepper
125g (4oz) blue cheese	

Place ingredients in a food processor or blender; pulse until well blended. Wrap in foil (see opposite). Place in the freezer until hard, about 45 minutes. To serve, roll back foil and cut into 1cm (½in) slices. When slicing from frozen, warm the knife through under hot water first. After slicing, always tightly re-wrap the unused flavoured butter roll in the foil before returning to refrigerator or freezer.

THINK AHEAD
Make up to 6 weeks in advance and refrigerate. Alternatively, make up to 9 months in advance and place in freezer. To keep sliced butter chilled outdoors, float slices in a bowl of cold water and ice.

VARIATION
BLACK OLIVE BUTTER

MAKES 15 SERVINGS

Replace blue cheese with 100g (3½oz) stoned black olives, chopped. Add 3 tbsp thyme leaves and 1 tsp salt. Reduce black pepper by 1 tsp.

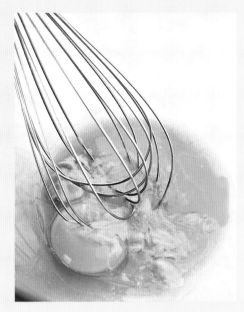

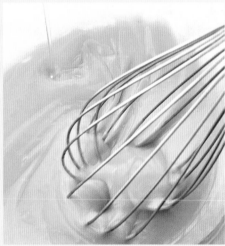

MAKING MAYONNAISE
Whisk the yolks until thick and creamy.

Add the oil in a steady stream.

MAYONNAISE

MAKES 300ml (10floz)
2 egg yolks
1 tsp creamy dijon mustard
1 tbsp red wine vinegar
½ tsp salt
pinch black pepper
150ml (5floz) sunflower oil
150ml (5floz) olive oil

Make sure that all the ingredients are at room temperature before you begin. Set a deep bowl on a cloth to prevent it from slipping as you whisk. Whisk the egg yolks, mustard, vinegar, salt and pepper together in a bowl until thick and creamy, 1 minute (see opposite).
Combine the oils in a jug. Whisk the oil into the egg yolk mixture a drop at a time until it thickens (see opposite). Add the remaining oil in a thin, steady stream, whisking constantly until thick and glossy. Whisk in any flavouring, if using, according to recipe variations opposite. Adjust seasoning, adding more mustard, vinegar, salt or pepper to taste.

THINK AHEAD
Make mayonnaise up to 3 days in advance. Cover and refrigerate. Return to room temperature before stirring to prevent the mayonnaise from separating.

COOKS' NOTE
If the ingredients are too cold or the oil is added too quickly, the mayonnaise may separate. Don't throw it away! Combine 1 tsp vinegar and 1 tsp creamy dijon mustard in a clean bowl. Whisk in the separated mayonnaise drop by drop until the mixture re-emulsifies.

USING READY MADE MAYONNAISE

Use ready made mayonnaise when in need of a time saving short-cut or if health concerns are an issue for you. Seek out a good quality whole egg brand of mayonnaise and freshen the flavour by whisking in creamy dijon mustard, sugar and red wine vinegar or lemon juice to taste.

USING A MACHINE

Follow recipe for mayonnaise. Place the egg yolks, mustard, vinegar, salt, pepper and sugar with 3 tbsp of the oil in a food processor or blender; process until blended, 10 seconds. While the machine is running, pour in the remaining oil in a thin, steady stream, until the mixture emulsifies and becomes thick and glossy. Pulse in any flavouring, if using. Adjust seasoning, adding more mustard, vinegar, salt or pepper to taste.

COOKS' NOTE
If using a food processor, depending on its capacity, you may need to stop the machine at intervals to scrape down the sides and over the base of the bowl with a spatula.

SAFETY WARNING ON RAW EGGS
Because of potential risk of salmonella, pregnant women, young children and anyone with a weakened immune system should avoid eating raw eggs. Make sure you use only the freshest (preferably organic) eggs, and if in doubt, substitute ready made mayonnaise (see above).

ROAST RED PEPPER AÏOLI

MAKES 300ml (10floz)

2 red peppers
1 recipe mayonnaise (see page 142)

Grill, peel and seed the peppers (see page 160). Place in food processor or blender; pulse until smooth. Whisk pepper purée into the mayonnaise.

ROAST GARLIC AÏOLI

MAKES 300ml (10floz)

1 head of garlic
I recipe mayonnaise (see page 142)

Slice off top of garlic, cutting through the cloves. Place cut-side up in oven tray. Drizzle over olive oil and sprinkle with salt and pepper. Preheat oven to 150°C (300°F) gas 2. Roast garlic head until completely soft, 1 hour. Leave to cool. Squeeze out cloves from papery skins. Mash until smooth. Whisk into mayonnaise.

CHILLI LIME MAYONNAISE

MAKES 300ml (10floz)

1 fresh green chilli, seeded and
  finely chopped
1 tbsp finely chopped fresh coriander
1 tbsp lime juice
1 recipe mayonnaise (see page 142)

Whisk chilli, coriander and lime juice into mayonnaise.

SALADS & SIDES

SLOW ROAST TOMATO SALAD

SERVES 4

6 tomatoes, halved
2 garlic cloves, finely sliced
1 tsp runny honey
1 tbsp balsamic vinegar
1 tbsp olive oil
salt, black pepper
1 tbsp chopped flat-leaf parsley
extra balsamic vinegar and
  olive oil to drizzle

Preheat oven to 150°C (300°F) gas 2. Place tomato halves cut side up in an oven tray. Place a garlic slice on top of each half. Drizzle over honey, vinegar and oil. Sprinkle with salt and pepper. Roast until very soft and lightly charred, 1 hour. Sprinkle with parsley and drizzle with oil and vinegar. Serve chilled or at room temperature

THINK AHEAD
Roast tomatoes up to 1 day in advance. Cover and refrigerate.

PARSLEY, MINT AND BULGUR SALAD WITH LEMON

SERVES 4

200g (7oz) bulgur wheat
200ml (7floz) boiling water
juice of 3 lemons
4 tbsp olive oil
2 tsp salt
1 tsp black pepper
1 tsp ground sumaq (optional)
4 medium tomatoes, seeded and diced
3 handfuls flat-leaf parsley leaves, roughly chopped
1 handful fresh mint leaves, torn

Place the bulgur wheat in a bowl. Pour over boiling water. Set aside until swollen and tender, 30 minutes. Drain well, pressing to squeeze out excess water. Return to the bowl. Pour over the lemon juice and oil. Add salt, pepper and sumaq (if using). Add tomatoes, parsley and mint. Mix together until evenly combined. Serve chilled or at room temperature.

THINK AHEAD
Prepare ingredients as directed up to 1 day in advance, but do not mix. Cover and refrigerate. Mix up to 1 hour before serving.

COOKS' NOTE
Sumaq is a dark burgundy coloured seed with a distinctive citrus tang often used in Lebanese, Iranian and Syrian cuisine. You can buy it in powdered form from Middle-Eastern stores or by mail-order (see page 167). It gives this refreshing, lemony salad an extra kick, but is not essential.

CREAMY POTATO SALAD WITH CELERY AND CHIVES

SERVES 4

750g (1½ lb) new potatoes, cut
  into bite-size pieces
1 tsp creamy dijon mustard
1 tbsp red wine vinegar
2 tbsp olive oil
1 tsp salt
½ tsp black pepper
125g (4oz) cream cheese
150ml (5floz) greek-style yoghurt
  or crème fraîche
2 celery sticks, finely diced
2½ tbsp finely chopped fresh chives
extra snipped fresh chives to garnish

Place potatoes in a large pan of cold
water. Bring to the boil. Gently simmer
until tender when pierced with the tip of
a knife, but still firm, 10-15 minutes.
Drain.

In large bowl, mix mustard, vinegar, oil,
salt and pepper until smooth. Add hot
potatoes. Toss gently to coat each potato
piece. Set aside for 30 minutes to allow
flavours to combine.

Beat cream cheese and yoghurt or crème
fraîche until smooth. Stir in celery and
chives. Mix gently with potatoes to coat
evenly. Add salt and pepper to taste.
Refrigerate for at least 1 hour before
serving. Garnish with extra chives. Serve
chilled or at room temperature.

THINK AHEAD
Make salad up to 1 day in advance. Cover and
refrigerate.

COOKS' NOTE
If you can't find fresh chives, spring onions are also
excellent in this creamy, crunchy potato salad.

SESAME SOBA NOODLE SALAD

SERVES 4

2 tbsp sesame seeds
250g (8oz) soba noodles
3 tbsp shoyu (japanese soy sauce)
1 tbsp sesame oil

Toast sesame seeds in a dry pan over a low heat until nutty and lightly coloured,
5 minutes. Set aside. Cook noodles in a large pan of boiling water until tender but
firm, 5 minutes. Drain and rinse in cold water to cool completely. Drain again. Place
in a bowl. Add toasted seeds, shoyu and oil. Mix gently to coat noodles. Serve
chilled or at room temperature

THINK AHEAD
Prepare salad up to 6 hours in advance. Cover and refrigerate.

COOKS' NOTE
Soba noodles are made from buckwheat flour. These greyish-brown Japanese noodles are available from Asian
stores, healthfood shops and most supermarkets. Alternatively, use Chinese egg noodles.

ORIENTAL NOODLE SALAD WITH CORIANDER AND LIME

SERVES 4

250g (8oz) rice vermicelli noodles
1 medium carrot, diagonally sliced,
  then cut into fine strips
¼ cucumber, diagonally sliced,
  then cut into fine strips
4 spring onions, diagonally sliced
2 fresh red chillies, seeded and
  finely sliced

2 tbsp chopped fresh coriander
  leaves
2 tbsp torn fresh mint leaves

FOR DRESSING
4 tbsp lime juice
4 tbsp fish sauce
2 tsp granulated sugar

Cook the noodles in a large pan of boiling water until tender but firm, 5 minutes.
Drain, then rinse in cold water to cool completely. Drain again. Roughly snip
noodles into smaller lengths with kitchen scissors.

For dressing, mix lime juice, fish sauce and sugar until sugar dissolves. Gently toss
noodles, carrot, cucumber, spring onion, chilli, coriander and mint with dressing
until well mixed. Serve chilled or at room temperature.

THINK AHEAD
Prepare noodles, salad ingredients and dressing up to 6 hours in advance. Store separately, covered and
refrigerated. Combine ingredients up to 1 hour before serving. Cover and refrigerate.

SMOKY BLACK BEAN SALAD

SERVES 4

250g (8oz) dried black beans
  or 2 - 400g (14oz) tins black beans,
  drained and rinsed

FOR DRESSING

2 garlic cloves, crushed
1 chipotle chilli, seeded and finely
  chopped or 1 tsp chilli powder
½ tsp ground cumin
½ tsp ground coriander
2 tsp salt
1 tsp black pepper
3 tbsp red wine vinegar
4 tbsp olive oil
1 recipe salsa fresca (see page 133)
6 tbsp crumbled feta cheese

If using dried beans, place in a large pan
with cold water to cover by 5cm (2in).
Bring to the boil. Boil hard for 10
minutes. Lower heat and simmer until
the beans are tender, 1-1½ hours. If
necessary, add hot water to keep beans
covered throughout the cooking time.
Drain thoroughly and set aside.

For dressing, combine garlic, chipotle or
chilli powder, cumin, coriander, salt,
pepper, vinegar and oil. If using dried
beans, pour dressing over hot cooked
beans. If using tinned beans, place dressing in a small pan, bring to the boil and
pour hot dressing over rinsed tinned
beans. Mix gently to coat beans. Add
salt, pepper and more chilli powder to
taste. Set aside for 30 minutes to allow
flavours to combine.

Pour salsa fresca over beans. Sprinkle
with feta. Serve chilled or at room
temperature.

THINK AHEAD
Dress beans up to 1 day in advance. Cover and
refrigerate. Top with salsa and cheese up to 1 hour
before serving.

COOKS' NOTE
You can also use red kidney, black-eyed or pinto beans
for this recipe.

SPICY PITTA CHIPS

SERVES 4
4 pitta breads
6 tbsp olive oil
4 garlic cloves
½ tsp crushed chilli flakes
1 tsp dried oregano
1 tsp dried thyme
½ tsp salt
¼ tsp black pepper

Split pitta breads open into two. Combine oil, garlic, chilli, oregano, thyme, salt and pepper. Brush crumb sides of pitta halves with spicy oil. Grill or bake according to instructions below. Remove to a wire rack and leave to cool. Break into large pieces and serve.

OUTDOOR	INDOOR
Grill over medium-hot coals until golden brown, 1-2 minutes per side.	Preheat oven to 180°C (350°F) gas 4. Place oiled side up on baking sheet. Toast until golden brown, 5-8 minutes.

CRISPY GREEN LEAF SALAD

SERVES 4
1 iceberg lettuce heart, quartered
125ml (4floz) blue cheese, honey mustard or creamy chive dressing (see opposite)
salt, black pepper

Arrange the lettuce quarters on a platter and spoon over the dressing. Sprinkle with salt and pepper. Serve chilled or at room temperature.

COOKS' NOTE
Cos and Romaine lettuce hearts are also delicious with any of these dressings.

CREAMY CHIVE DRESSING

MAKES 125ml (4floz)
1 tbsp finely chopped fresh chives
2 tsp creamy dijon mustard
1 tsp granulated sugar
1 tbsp lemon juice
2 tbsp olive oil
8 tbsp greek-style yoghurt or crème fraîche
salt, black pepper

Mix together chives, mustard, sugar, lemon juice, oil and yoghurt or crème fraîche until thick and smooth. Add salt and pepper to taste.

THINK AHEAD
Make dressing up to 1 day in advance. Cover and refrigerate.

HONEY MUSTARD DRESSING

MAKES 125ml (4floz)
1 garlic clove, crushed
1 tbsp runny honey
2 tbsp creamy dijon mustard
2 tbsp red wine vinegar
4 tbsp olive oil
2 tbsp crème fraîche or sour cream
salt, black pepper

Mix together garlic, honey, mustard, vinegar, oil and crème fraîche or sour cream until thick and smooth. Add salt and pepper to taste.

THINK AHEAD
Make dressing up to 1 day in advance. Cover and refrigerate.

BLUE CHEESE DRESSING

MAKES 125ml (4floz)
4 tbsp blue cheese, crumbled
1 tbsp finely chopped spring onions
2 tbsp red wine vinegar
2 tbsp sour cream
4 tbsp olive oil
salt, black pepper

Mix together blue cheese, spring onion, vinegar, sour cream and oil until combined. Add salt and pepper to taste.

THINK AHEAD
Make dressing up to 1 day in advance. Cover and refrigerate.

MAKING FOCACCIA DOUGH
Knead the dough until it is smooth, light and and elastic.

Cover the dough with a cloth and leave to rise until doubled in size.

FOCACCIA

SERVES 4 - 6

500g (1lb) strong white flour
2 tsp salt
325ml (11floz) tepid water
2 tsp dried yeast

2 tbsp olive oil
2 tsp fresh rosemary leaves
salt and pepper to sprinkle

Place the flour in a bowl. Make a well in the middle and sprinkle the salt around the edges. Pour the water into the well and sprinkle over the yeast. Leave for 5 minutes to allow the yeast to soften, then stir to dissolve. Add olive oil to the mixture.

Draw in the rest of the flour to make a rough, sticky dough. Turn out on to a lightly floured surface and knead for 10 minutes, until smooth, light and elastic (see opposite). Put back into the bowl, cover with a cloth and leave until doubled in size, about 1½ hours (see opposite).

Preheat the oven to 200°C (400°F) Gas 6. Deflate the dough by pressing down with the palm of your hand. Roll out into a flat round about 23cm (9in) across and place on an oiled baking sheet. Sprinkle with rosemary leaves, salt and pepper, or top according to the variations below. Cover with a cloth and leave until risen, about 30 minutes. Bake until bread is puffed and crisp on top, about 30 minutes. Cool on a wire rack. Serve warm, sprinkled with coarse salt and cut into wedges.

THINK AHEAD
Make and knead the dough and leave to rise in the refrigerator for 8-12 hours. Leave to stand at room temperature for half an hour before knocking back and shaping again. Rise again and bake according to the recipe. Alternatively, bake focaccia 1 day in advance and reheat in a hot oven for 15 minutes.

POTATO FOCACCIA WITH THYME

SERVES 4 - 6

1 recipe unbaked
  focaccia dough (see above)

FOR TOPPING

500g (1lb) baby potatoes
125g (4oz) gruyère cheese, grated
2 tsp fresh thyme leaves
4 tbsp crème fraîche

Prepare dough according to recipe above. Leave to rise through the second step. Preheat the oven to 200°C (400°F) gas 6. Cut potatoes into 0.5cm (¼in) slices. Bring a pan of salted water to the boil, add the potatoes, bring back to the boil and cook until the centres are just tender when pricked, about 5 minutes. Drain well and cool.
Shape dough according to the third step in the recipe above. Sprinkle half the cheese on top of the shaped dough. Arrange the potato slices over cheese. Scatter over remaining cheese. Sprinkle with thyme, salt and pepper. Dot potatoes with crème fraîche.
Bake until bread is puffed and topping is crisp, about 30 minutes.

ROAST ONION FOCACCIA WITH ROSEMARY

SERVES 4 - 6

1 recipe unbaked focaccia dough
  (see above)

FOR TOPPING

3 red onions, cut into wedges
1 tbsp olive oil
125g (4oz) gruyère cheese, grated
2 tsp chopped fresh rosemary leaves
salt, black pepper

Prepare dough according to recipe above. Leave to rise through the second step. Preheat the oven to 200°C (400°F) gas 6. Place onions in an oven tray. Drizzle with oil. Roast until soft and wilted, 30 minutes. Cool.
Shape dough according to the third step in the recipe above. Sprinkle half the cheese evenly on top of the shaped dough. Arrange onions over cheese. Scatter over remaining cheese. Sprinkle with rosemary, salt and pepper.
Bake until bread is puffed and topping is crisp, about 30 minutes.

THE MENUS

NUEVO TEX MEX

A real crowd-pleaser: south of the border classics meet fresher, bolder flavours for great, gutsy food. Everyone will love this fun fiesta of wraps, chips, salsas and dips. Icy cold beers, please!

Creamy Avocado Salsa
(see page 132)
Store-bought tortilla chips

•

Spicy Lime Chicken Wings
(see page 101)
Chargrilled Quesadillas with
Spicy Coriander
(see page 128)

•

Spiced Beef Fajitas with Salsa
Fresca and Guacamole
(see page 38)
Smoky Black Bean Salad
(see page 151)

•

Premium brand chocolate ice-cream

DISTINCTLY MOORISH

Aromatic spices, fragrant herbs and refreshing citrus flavours make this Morrocan-inspired menu a delight for all the senses.

Honey Harissa Kofte
(see page 60)
Spiced Chickpea Sauce
(see page 137)
Spicy Pitta Chips
(see page 152)

•

Coriander Lamb Pitta Wraps
(see page 58)
Parsley, Mint and Bulgur Salad
with Lemon
(see page 147)

•

Grill Roast Sweet
Spiced Oranges
(see page 126)

VEGETARIAN FEAST

As the vegetables come hot off the grill, arrange them on large platters, spoon over the sauces and let everyone help themselves. You can make the focaccia and sauces a day ahead; refer to our THINK AHEAD *notes.*

Creamy Blue Cheese Sauce
(see page 133)
Spicy Pitta Chips
(see page 152)

•

Chargrilled Aubergine Slices
with Lemon Tahini Sauce
(see page 122)
Chargilled Courgettes with
Roast Pepper and Basil Salsa
(see page 123)
Chargrilled New Potato Skewers
(see page 120)
Roast Onion Focaccia with
Rosemary
(see page 155)

BARBECUE ON THE BEACH

A beach is, of course, not essential. The backyard will do, but plenty of lemon wedges and paper napkins are a must. We suggest a well-chilled crisp white wine to accompany this celebration of seafood.

Clams in Coriander Chilli Butter
(see page 74)
Squid with Tomato Avocado Salsa
(see page 69)

•

Provençal Seafood Grillade with
Lemon Fennel Dressing and Roast
Garlic Aïoli
(see page 86)
A crusty baguette

•

Bowlful of summer berries

REAL FAST MENU FOR ENTERTAINING

High-flavour, low-input dishes for the time-challenged cook. You can make this menu a last-minute affair or use our THINK AHEAD *notes if you prefer to plan in advance.*

Honey Soy Chicken Wings
(see page 101)
Spicy Peanut Sauce
(see page 136)

•

Rosemary Peppered Pork Chops
(see page 44)
Chargrilled Tomatoes
(see page 120)
Crispy Green Leaf Salad with
Creamy Chive Dressing
(see page 152)

•

Chargrilled Nectarines
(see page 125)
Premium brand vanilla ice-cream

ISLAND BARBECUE

A totally tropical menu. Warm spices, hot chilli, savoury seasonings and a dash of dark rum will bring the sunny flavours of the Caribbean to your backyard.

Lemon Chilli Prawns
(see page 66)
Pineapple Lime Salsa
(see page 134)

•

Skewered Bajun Chicken
(see page 96)
Chargrilled Squash with Jerked Honey Rum Glaze
(see page 123)
Chargilled Corn on the Cob with Coriander Chilli butter
(see page 119)

•

Grill Roast Cinnamon Rum Bananas
(see page 126)
Premium brand vanilla ice-cream

ASIAN FUSION

Eastern traditions meet western trends in this simple, fresh and stylish menu bursting with vibrant flavours.

Spicy Masala Prawns
(see page 64)
Thai Spiced Chicken Wings
(see page 100)
Coriander Coconut Sauce
(see page 138)

•

Spiced Soy Duck
(see page 113)
Sesame Soba Noodle Salad
(see page 148)
Fresh Papaya Sambal
(see page 137)

•

Platter of chilled fresh tropical fruit

TUSCAN GRILL

A great menu if cooking for a crowd. You can bake the focaccia, prepare the lamb and grill the bruschetta and peppers a day ahead. A rich and rustic red wine perfectly complements this sensational sun-drenched menu.

Char-Roast Lemon Oregano Peppers on Bruschetta
(see page 129)

•

Lamb with Anchovy, Prosciutto and Parsley **(see page 54)**
Slow Roast Tomato Salad
(see page 147)
Potato Focaccia with Thyme
(see page 155)

•

Grill Roast Honey Orange Figs
(see page 126)

NOUVELLE GRILL

A thoroughly modern menu that combines global influences with contemporary inspirations.

Radish Tzatziki
(see page 135)
Spicy Pitta Chips
(see page 152)

•

Prawns with Tamarind Recado
(see page 67)
Pineapple Lime Salsa
(see page 134)

•

Spice-crusted Tuna with Thai Citrus Dressing
(see page 78)
Oriental Noodle Salad with Coriander and Lime
(see page 150)

•

Grill Roast Lemon Liqueur Strawberries
(see page 126)

NEW AMERICAN GRILL

A new look at patio cuisine! All the family favourites - drums, ribs and steaks with the influence of Asian and Latin flavours to replace the standard barbecue sauce. Our potato salad is as creamy as Mom's, but we make it lighter to suit today's tastes.

Honey Mustard Chicken Drumsticks
(see page 102)
Spiced Hoisin Ribs
(see page 48)

•

Chargrilled T-bone Steak with Chimi Churri Sauce
(see page 34)
Chargrilled Tomatoes
(see page 120)
Creamy Potato Salad with Celery and Chives
(see page 148)

•

Premium brand vanilla ice-cream

NOTES FROM THE COOKS ON INGREDIENTS

ACHIOTE SEASONING is a Mexican spice blend of ground annatto seeds, oregano, cumin, cinnamon, pepper and cloves. It is available powdered or as a paste from mail order or speciality stores (see page 167), or you can make your own (see page 23).

ANNATTO, also called achiote (see page 23), are the rusty red seeds of the annatto tree. Annatto is known as the saffron of Latin America, where it is used for its brick red colour and earthy flavour.

CAPERS are the pickled bud of the caper plant. Always drain well before using.

CARAWAY SEEDS are aromatic seeds with a nutty, mildly anise flavour, widely used in Central European baking and cooking.

CARDAMOM is best used freshly ground as its fragrance diminishes with time. Crush lightly, open, discard the pods and grind the seeds (see page 161). If you are buying cardamom in the pod, choose green not brown cardamom for the recipes in this book.

CHILLI (see page 18) comes fresh, as powder or as flakes. There are over 200 different varieties of fresh chillies, varying in colour, size, shape and heat. When buying fresh chillies, make sure the stem is still on and that it is as fresh as possible; avoid any that have no stem. As a general rule, the smaller the chilli the hotter it is. Capsaicin, the substance in chillies responsible for their heat, can cause a very painful burning sensation if it comes into contact with the eyes or areas of sensitive skin. Make sure you wash your hands thoroughly after handling chillies. To reduce the level of heat, remove the seeds before using (see page 160). **Scotch bonnets** are fresh, lantern-shaped chillies from the Caribbean with a fruity, citrus flavour and fiery heat. If

you can't find them fresh, use Carribbean hot pepper sauce as an alternative and add drop by drop to taste. **Chilli powder** is a hot seasoning of ground dried chillies, garlic, oregano, cumin and coriander. Pure chilli powders are ground from one variety of chilli without the additon of other spices and flavourings. **Ancho chilli powder** is made from ground dried poblano chillies from the Americas. It is deep reddish brown in colour with a mildly pungent, rich, sun-dried flavour. **Kashmiri chilli powder** is made from powdered Kashmiri chillies from India; it has a sweetish, pungent flavour without a burning heat. **Chipotles in Adobo** are dried smoked jalapeño chillies, pickled and tinned in a piquant sauce made from chillies, herbs and vinegar. They are available by mail order or from speciality stores (see page 167).

CHILLI SAUCE is available in many different varieties. We use two types, and both can be found in large supermarkets or in Asian stores. **Chinese hot chilli sauce** (see page 18) is made from chillies, salt and vinegar; use chilli sauce as an alternative. **Thai sweet chilli sauce** (see page 19), flavoured with ginger and garlic as well as sugar, salt, vinegar and chillies, is often labelled "dipping sauce for chicken". If you can't find it, make your own. Combine 150ml (5floz) rice or cider vinegar with 4 tbsp granulated sugar in a small pan; stir to dissolve. Bring to the boil and simmer until syrupy, 5 minutes. Stir in ¼ tsp salt, 1 finely chopped garlic clove, ½ tsp grated ginger and 1 seeded and finely chopped red chilli. Cool before using. Cover and refrigerate for up to 1 week.

CHIPOTLES IN ADOBO (see chillies)

COCONUT MILK is available in tins from Asian stores and large supermarkets. Shake well before opening.

FISH SAUCE (see page 19) is thin, salty, brown sauce made from fermented fish and used extensively in Southeast Asian cooking. It is available from large supermarkets, Asian stores or mail order (see page 167). We use Thai fish sauce called nam pla; use soy sauce as an alternative.

FIVE-SPICE POWDER is a Chinese spice blend of ground cloves, cinnamon, fennel, star anise and Szechwan pepper.

GINGER in its fresh form has a very different flavour from ground. Do not substitute ground ginger for fresh. Wrap and store fresh ginger in the refrigerator for up to 3 weeks. Cut off the skin with a sharp knife before grating (see page 160). **Pickled ginger** (see page 20) is the Japanese condiment for sushi. It is easily recognised by its pink colour and is available in jars.

GREEK-STYLE YOGHURT is made from cow's or ewe's milk and is rich, creamy and flavourful. Use half sour cream and half whole milk yoghurt as an alternative.

HOISIN SAUCE (see page 20) is a slightly sweet, thick, dark brown sauce made from soy beans, garlic, and spices. It will keep indefinitely in a covered jar.

LEMON GRASS (see page 21) comes in long stalks and has a fragrant citrus flavour and aroma. Use only the tender inner stem as the the outer leaves are tough. Lemon grass freezes very well, so you can buy it in quantity, freeze and use it as needed. As an alternative, use ½ tsp each of grated lime and lemon zest for 1 lemon grass stalk.

MIRIN is Japanese rice wine. It is sweeter than sake and used only for cooking. Use medium dry sherry as an alternative.

MISO (see page 20) is Japanese fermented soy bean paste. It is salty but highly nutritious. It is available in Asian stores, health food stores and large supermarkets. It comes in various colours and keeps indefinitely in the refrigerator.

MUSTARD comes in many forms, but we prefer to use smooth and creamy French Dijon. For a coarser texture, use grainy Dijon mustard.

PANCETTA is flavourful Italian streaky bacon. Store wrapped in the refrigerator for up to 3 weeks. Use streaky bacon as an alternative.

PEPPER should be freshly ground or cracked for maximum flavour. A good pepper grinder is an essential item for any cook who values flavour.

POMEGRANATE MOLASSES (see page 20) - also referred to as syrup or concentrate - is made by boiling down pomegranate juice to a thick, dark brown liquid with a distinctive sweet-sour flavour. It's a favourite flavouring across the Middle East, but especially in Iran, Syria and Lebanon. It is available in bottles from Middle-Eastern stores or by gourmet mail order (see page 167). Date molasses, which is readily found in healthfood stores, can be used as an alternative.

PRESERVED LEMONS are whole lemons pickled in salty lemon juice and used as a flavouring and condiment in Moroccan cooking.

PROSCIUTTO is Italian raw ham that has been seasoned, salt-cured and air-dried.

RICE NOODLES are Asian noodles made from rice flour. Use Chinese dried egg noodles as an alternative. Cook according to the package instructions.

SAKE is Japan's famous rice wine, widely used as a flavouring in Japanese sauces and marinades. Use dry sherry as an alternative.

SALT should always be sea salt, whether coarse or fine. The quality of salt matters. Different salts have different flavours and different degrees of saltiness. Salt draws out the moisture in meat, so we always season with it only after grilling.

SCOTCH BONNETS
(see chillies)

SESAME OIL (see page 20) is best when it is one of the Asian brands, and is extracted from toasted sesame seeds. Don't confuse this with the lighter sesame oil with a less intense flavour that is sold in healthfood stores.

SOBA NOODLES are very fine Japanese buckwheat noodles, available in Asian stores, healthfood stores and large supermarkets. Use Chinese dried egg noodles as an alternative. Cook according to the package instructions.

SOY SAUCE is a major seasoning in Asian cooking. It is available in a number of varieties, ranging in colour and flavour. We use light soy sauce when we wish to preserve the colour of the food but dark soy sauce has a richer flavour. **Japanese soy sauce**, called **shoyu**, is sweeter, lighter and less salty; use light soy sauce as an alternative.

SPICES should be bought whole and toasted and ground yourself, for the best flavour (see page 161). Even if you store them for a month or so, your home-ground spices will still be more flavourful than anything you buy ready ground from the supermarket.

TAHINI is a paste made from grinding roasted sesame seeds. It is sold in jars in large supermarkets, healthfood and Middle-Eastern stores. Shake well before using.

TAMARIND (see page 20) has a bright, sharp, tangy flavour. It is used mostly in Southeast Asian and Middle-Eastern cooking. It is available as jars of paste or concentrate or in blocks of sticky pulp. To use the pulp, dissolve in boiling water and sieve out the seeds: use ½ cup pulp to 1 cup water for a thick paste. It will keep in the refrigerator for up to 3 days, or you can freeze it in ice cube trays.

Tamarind pulp and paste are available from Asian, Middle-Eastern and Hispanic stores, or by gourmet mail order (see page 167). Use freshly squeezed lime juice as an alternative.

VINEGAR comes in a variety of forms. **Red wine vinegar** (see page 21) and **white wine vinegar** have different flavours and levels of acidity and should not be used interchangeably. **Balsamic vinegar** (see page 21) is a widely available Italian vinegar; it is dark in colour with a sweet, pungent flavour. **Cider vinegar** is a mellow, fruity vinegar made from apple cider. **Rice vinegar** (see page 21) with its subtly sweet, mellow flavour, is used extensively in Japanese cooking. It is available in Asian stores and health-food stores. Cider vinegar can be used as an alternative.

WASABI is a pungent green horseradish used in Japanese cuisine. It is available in dried powder form in tins and as a paste in tubes (see page 20). Use horseradish sauce as an alternative.

WHITE TRUFFLE OIL has a rich, earthy flavour and aroma and is delicious drizzled on pasta, risotto, vegetables and salads. It is available in small bottles from speciality or Italian stores, or from gourmet mail order sources (see page 167).

ESSENTIAL SKILLS

GRILLING AND PEELING PEPPERS
Grill peppers over a hot outdoor flame or under a preheated indoor grill. Turn as needed until blackened on all sides, 10-15 minutes. Place in a plastic bag or a bowl with a plate on top and allow them to cool. Peel off the skin using the tip of a small knife. Cut the peppers into quarters and remove the core. Scrape away seeds and discard.

PEELING A GARLIC CLOVE
Set the flat side of the knife on top and strike it with your fist. This action will loosen the skin, allowing it to peel away easily by using your fingers. Discard the skin.

REMOVING SEEDS FROM A CHILLI
Halve the chillies lengthwise with a small, sharp knife. Scape out the seeds and cut away the white ribs from each half. Wash hands after handling chillies.

CHOPPING AN ONION
Peel the onion, leaving the root end on. Cut the onion in half and lay one half, cut side down, on a chopping board. With a sharp knife cut horizontally towards the root end, and then vertically. Be sure to cut just to the root but not through it. Finally, cut the onion crosswise into diced pieces.

GRATING FRESH GINGER
Use a sharp knife or vegetable peeler to cut away the skin from the ginger root. Grate the ginger, making sure to grate with the grain and not against it.

GRINDING WHOLE SPICES

Whole spices may be ground or cracked by hand in a mortar. Alternatively, to coarse grind or crack spices, place them in a plastic zip-lock bag and crush them with rolling pin or heavy saucepan. For large quantities, use a blender or food processor.

TOASTING SPICES

Place a dry cast iron pan over a medium-hot heat until hot, 2 minutes. Add the spices and toast, shaking the pan, until the spices are dark and aromatic, 5 minutes. Remove from pan and cool.

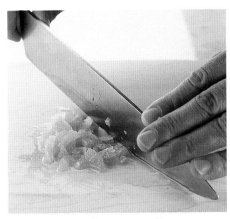

PEELING AND CHOPPING CITRUS

Cut a slice from the top and the bottom of the fruit. Cut away the rind, pith and skin, working from top to bottom and following the curve of the fruit. Slice the peeled fruit crosswise into 0.5cm (¼in) slices. Stack and chop the slices finely.

SEEDING TOMATOES

Cut the tomato in half crosswise. Gently squeeze each tomato half, pushing out the seeds with your fingertip.

MAKING CITRUS WEDGES

Cut the fruit in half lengthwise. Place cut side down on a board. Trim the stalk ends and discard. Cut each half across into 4 wedges.

INDEX

Index compiled by Valerie Lewis Chandler

AUTHORS' ACKNOWLEDGEMENTS

We would like to thank:
Our three very special teams, who are, if you like, the rocks on which this enterprise is built.
The Books for Cooks team, but especially Victoria Blashford Snell, Jennifer Joyce, Kimiko Barber and Ursula Ferrigno. Their passion for food, both contemporary and traditional, remains a constant inspiration and we are eternally grateful for their willingness to share their discoveries with us.

The Covent Garden team, Stuart Jackman, Julia Pemberton Hellums, and Sally Somers for being just so fast, just so flexible, just so ready to do it! But perhaps this book really belongs to the studio team and especially Ian O'Leary, for being ready, willing and able to get out of the studio into the big outdoors. Things began pleasantly enough down on the farm in the late summer sunshine, but we had to work our way through a four seasons' worth of weather to arrive at that bitterly cold day in December in our back garden.
Photography in torrential rain was never so much fun.

MAIL ORDER SOURCES

THE SPICE SHOP
1 Blenheim Crescent,
London W11 2EE
T: 020-7221-4448
Mail Order. Herbs, spices, seasonings, condiments and ethnic ingredients from around the world, including chipotles in adobo, tamarind concentrate, achiote seasoning and pomegranate molasses.

CUCINA DIRECT
PO Box 6611, London SW15 2WG
T: 020-8246-4300
www.cucinadirect.co.uk
Catalogue available. Tools for the cook, including heavy duty tongs, ridged cast iron grill pans and hinged grill racks.

SELFRIDGES
400 Oxford Street, London W1 1AB
T: 020-7318-3895 (food hall direct line)
www.selfridges.co.uk
Delivery Service (£50 minimum order).
Selfridges Food Hall stocks luxury foods and speciality ingredients from around the world, including pomegranate molasses. Also comprehensive kitchenware department.

Australia
BBQs R US
660 Whithorse Rd, Mitcham
Melbourne, Victoria
T: 9873 1444
www.bbqrus.com.au
Extensive range of barbecue grills and accessories, including commercial models and special models that are custom made to order. Other outlets in Fairfield, Cheltenham, Footscray, Seaford and Mornington Peninsula.

HERBIE'S SPICES
745 Darling St, Rozelle
Sydney, NSW 2039
T: 02 9555 6035
www.herbie@herbies.com.au
Mail order. Comprehensive range of herbs, spices and seasonings, including pomegranate molasses.

THE VITAL INGREDIENT
206 Clarendon St
South Melbourne, Victoria 3205
T: 9696 3511
Gourmet ingredients and kitchenware.

THE ESSENTIAL INGREDIENT
4 Australia St, PO Box 398
Camperdown, Sydney, NSW 2050
T: 02 9550 5477
Email: essential@loom.net.au
Mail Order. 2,000 food products available, including chipotles in adobo. Comprehensive range of cookware.

BARBECUES GALORE*
84 stores across Australia
Call 13 12 54 to speak to your nearest store
www.barbequesgalore.com.au
Extensive range of barbecue grill accessories. Offers expert advice to ensure successful barbecue grilling.

KAKULAS BROS
185 William St, Northbridge
Perth, WA 6003
T: 08 9328 5285
Fax: 08 9328 2761
Excellent range of Middle Eastern, Indian and European herbs and spices.

AMANO
12 Station St, Cottesloe
Perth, WA 6011
T: 08 9384 0378
Perth's largest cooking school and store. Comprehensive range of cookware and speciality ingredients.

New Zealand
MOORE WILSON'S
Cnr Tory and College Sts
PO Box 6041, Wellington
T: 04 384 9906
email: taste&value@moorewilson.co.nz
Sauces and condiments from all around the world. Barbecue grill accessories. Other outlets in Porirua, Lower Hut and Masterton.

SABATO'S
57 Normanby Rd, Mt Eden, Auck
Tollfree: 0800 SABATO
www.sabato.co.nz
Catalogue available. European speciality foods, including smoked paprika.

HOW WE MAKE OUR BOOKS

In 1983, a tiny bookstore with a unique concept opened in London's Notting Hill. BOOKS FOR COOKS is a bookstore run by cooks for cooks, selling only cookbooks, teaching cooking classes, cooking from the books and serving up the results in a tiny restaurant among the bookshelves.

I work in the store, cook in the kitchen and teach in the school. It's true that I acquired my technical training as a professional chef, but, to my mind, my real culinary education began the day I crossed the threshold of BOOKS FOR COOKS. It's from my students and customers that I learn most about the way people live, cook and eat today, and it's this experience that informs the way we make our books. Real food for real life is our motto, and each title is specially devised to meet the needs of today's busy cooks.

I'm lucky enough to work in a team of dedicated food lovers. We research, test, photograph, write, design and edit our books from start to finish. All the ingredients are bought at ordinary shops and tested in a domestic kitchen. Our recipes are designed to be cooked at home. Oh yes, and it's all real food in the photographs!

You can write, phone, fax or e-mail us any time.

We'd love to hear from you.

Eric

BOOKS FOR COOKS
4 BLENHEIM CRESCENT
LONDON W11 1NN
TEL. 020-07221-1992
FAX. 020-07221-1517

info@booksforcooks.com

Quick & Clever
WATERCOLOUR LANDSCAPES
Charles Evans

David and Charles

This book is dedicated to the memory of Margaret Abbey, who is seen here sketching at Morston Quay. This was the last time I saw her at her happiest, on a painting holiday; it was a pleasure to have known her, and the world is a sadder place without her.

A DAVID & CHARLES BOOK
David & Charles is a subsidiary of F + W (UK) Ltd.,
an F + W Publications Inc. company

Copyright © Charles Evans 2005

Distributed in North America
by F + W Publications, Inc.
4700 East Galbraith Road
Cincinnati, OH 45236
1-800-289-0963

A catalogue record for this book is available from the British Library.

ISBN 0 7153 1931 0 hardback
ISBN 0 7153 1932 9 paperback (USA only)

Printed in China by SNP Leefung
for David & Charles
Brunel House   Newton Abbot   Devon

Commissioning Editor   Mic Cady
Desk Editor   Lewis Birchon
Project Editor   Ian Kearey
Art Editor   Ali Myer
Production Controller   Kelly Smith

Photography by Karl Adamson

Visit our website at www.davidandcharles.co.uk

David & Charles books are available from all good bookshops; alternatively you can contact our Orderline on (0)1626 334555 or write to us at FREEPOST EX2 110, David & Charles Direct, Newton Abbot, TQ12 4ZZ (no stamp required UK mainland).

Contents

Introduction

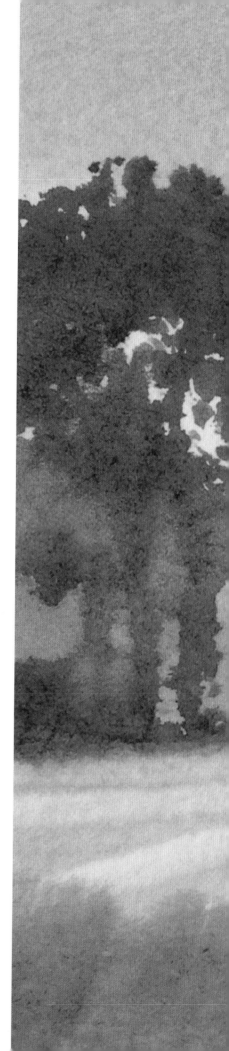

My kind of painting is not about fiddling or messing about with lots of complex processes and tiny brushes – it's about slapping on paint using big brushes, getting dirty and having fun. The point is that this is all supposed to be about fun and enjoyment; that's why we start painting.

The one thing I can promise in this book is that you won't be bogged down by technical jargon or confusing terms; instead, there will be words and phrases such as slap it on, a daub, squiggly bits and splat. This is about as technical as I usually get, although I have included a few more technical phrases so you can recognize them when you need to.

For what seems like over a hundred years, I have always had tremendous passion and enjoyment for my painting. People tell me, 'You always make it look so easy', but if you are using big brushes and having fun and slapping on the paint, then results certainly do come quickly and you have definitely enjoyed yourself; and that, remember, is what it's all about.

A quick look at the contents of this book will show that it's not the type where you have to start at the easy beginning and work your way through to the complex end, missing out sections at your peril. The name of the game is to get you painting the watercolour landscapes that you want to paint, so you can dip in and out as suits you best. (But that's not to say you can't work from beginning to end if you want, of course.)

The exercises are designed to be very quick and easy, and should help you build up the confidence to tackle the parts and details that people often find difficult – skies, boats, trees, people and animals, and buildings. The projects incorporate all the exercise themes, and also introduce new ideas and solutions that you can work with and use in your own paintings.

If you glean anything from this book, it will hopefully not be, as we are told so many times, that watercolours are the most difficult painting medium; it will be that they are the most enjoyable one, with the most instant effects. In addition, the usual trauma of making a mistake can be eased by the fact that this is not the ruination or the ending of the painting; if you blunder, simply wash it out and do it again. So sit back, relax – and enjoy.

Materials and Equipment

All the materials that I use are made by Daler-Rowney. It's usually the case that you tend to use what your superiors used before you, such as course tutors or college lecturers. So you stick with what you are used to. For me, allied to this is the fact that Daler-Rowney products have an exceptionally long tradition and were always used by the likes of the great J.M.W. Turner – which is good enough for me!

Whether or not you decide to use the same materials as I do, remember that part of the title of this book is 'quick'; the big rule here is not to burden yourself down with all sorts of stuff that you'll never use and that just gets in the way. Use the guidelines I've given in this section, keep equipment to a minimum, and you won't go far wrong.

Paint

The paints I use are all artists' quality: French ultramarine, burnt sienna, yellow ochre, raw umber, Hooker's green (dark), cerulean or cobalt blue, alizarin crimson and light red.

Three new paint colours are introduced for the first time in this book, the Charles Evans range: British sea, Mediterranean sea, and British sand, all produced by Daler-Rowney to my specifications. They are ready-mixed colours to make it easier for you to capture the colour of water: you can use them straight from the tubes or play around, mix and match and experiment.

The first two are called sea colours, but if you stick plenty of water in them, especially sea for Great Britain, this will do for any stretch of water, be it a lake or river. If you want to adjust the colour slightly, I would suggest adding a tiny touch of Hooker's green, which will change the colour sufficiently for a beautiful lake type of water that catches a hint of surrounding greenery.

Obviously, as with any other colour, these colours can be stronger or weaker depending on the amount of water added. Sea for the Mediterranean is a beautiful warm colour, and if you want to deepen it ever so slightly, to make it even more warm and strong, add a tiny tint of alizarin crimson – but it's just as good on its own, straight from the tube.

You can warm up the sand colour with the addition of a hint of burnt sienna, cool it down with a tiny touch of French ultramarine, or make it brighter with a similar amount of yellow ochre; for a very neutral beach, just use it straight from the tube.

Another very useful feature of the sand colour is that you can use it for mixing in place of white: when you mix white paint with a colour to make it lighter, you end up with an opaque colour because white is totally opaque – if you use the sand colour instead, its neutrality and transparency will lighten everything without making the mixed colour opaque.

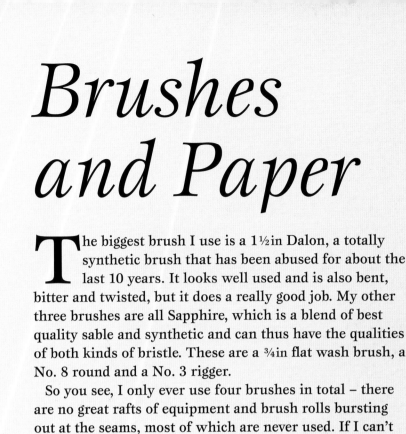

Brushes and Paper

The biggest brush I use is a 1½in Dalon, a totally synthetic brush that has been abused for about the last 10 years. It looks well used and is also bent, bitter and twisted, but it does a really good job. My other three brushes are all Sapphire, which is a blend of best quality sable and synthetic and can thus have the qualities of both kinds of bristle. These are a ¾in flat wash brush, a No. 8 round and a No. 3 rigger.

So you see, I only ever use four brushes in total – there are no great rafts of equipment and brush rolls bursting out at the seams, most of which are never used. If I can't hold it in my hand or keep it in my bucket, then it's surplus to requirements.

The paper I normally use, and have used throughout this book, is Langton Rough. This is only 300gsm (140lb) in weight, and both sides are identical – there's no wrong side, therefore, and you can't really go wrong with it. I never pre-stretch or mess about with the paper; I just chop a sheet in half and tape it to the board using ordinary masking tape.

Other Materials

T he 'lead' pencil that I use can be anything – basically, whatever I can nick from my nephew's chalkbox – because there is never, ever going to be be crosshatching or shading; I always just use a simple outline. The only time I do use fancy pencils is when I'm doing outdoor sketching, and for this I use a selection of Derwent watercolour pencils (see page 81).

My easel is a Westminster easel, which is metal. It is good and sturdy, and is well equipped to handle the rigours of airport luggage handlers. When I'm out on location and the wind is blowing, I simply pull out the rubber plugs at the bottom of the legs and whack the legs into the ground.

I use a hardback sketch book, A4 size. I stress the 'hardback' bit because the books are properly string bound, and therefore the pages don't fall out, no matter how much they are bashed. I always carry a penknife, because I never sharpen my pencils with a pencil sharpener.

My board is no more than a piece of MDF, smoothed and rounded at the edges. I use ordinary masking tape to stick the paper to the board.

And that's it – now let's get on with some painting!

Trees and Lake

This first project introduces my key ideas on
painting: keep paints and brushes to a minimum,
work fast and concentrate on the big picture.

Ideally, this little study should only take a few minutes to do. I used a limited number of colours, and I used the same mix for several parts of the painting. Most importantly, you should think about the overall picture all the time – don't get worried about whether anything is absolutely accurate or right, but work quickly and confidently.

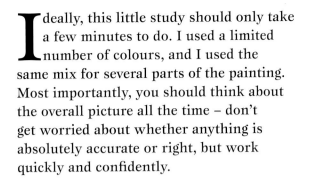

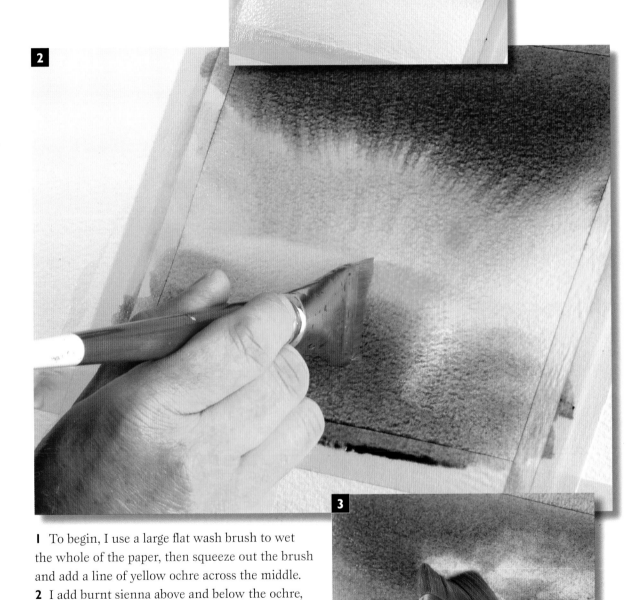

1 To begin, I use a large flat wash brush to wet the whole of the paper, then squeeze out the brush and add a line of yellow ochre across the middle.
2 I add burnt sienna above and below the ochre, and above and below that, a mix of French ultramarine with a tiny touch of burnt sienna. I mop up the bottom of the picture, squeeze the brush out and merge the colours.
3 After rinsing and squeezing out the brush, I draw out the pigment in the sky for clouds, and repeat this in the water for a reflection.

4 Using a really wet mix of French ultramarine and burnt sienna and a No. 8 round brush, I wipe the brush straight across the picture so that it spreads – bleeding of pigment is normally my worst enemy, but I can take advantage of it now. I repeat this in the water for the reflection of the trees in the distance. To make a difference between the water and the sky, I use the ¾in wash brush and clean water to suck out pigment in a line across the picture.

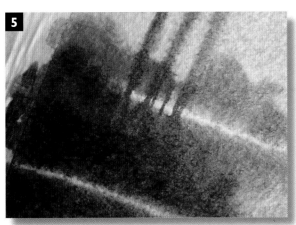

5 For the bushes, I make a watery mix of Hooker's green and burnt sienna, drop this on to the paper so that it spreads, and repeat below the dividing line. I then drop a mix of French ultramarine and burnt sienna into the green of the bushes to make shadows, and again repeat this, pulling out the colour in the reflections with the wash brush.

6 I now switch to a No. 3 rigger brush and use raw umber to make a couple of trees with their branches, repeating this for the reflections.

7 Returning to the round brush and the Hooker's green and burnt sienna mix, I dab on sharp-edged marks to make the foliage of the Scots pines. And that's it – the work only took me a couple of minutes to do, but it looks fine.

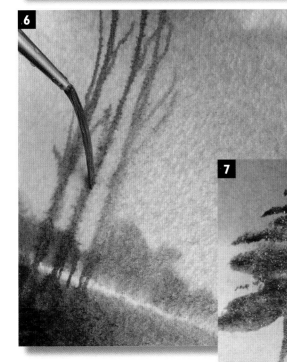

EXERCISE
SKIES

Whether it's a flat, open prairie or a crowded town scene with high buildings, any landscape needs to have an effective, convincing sky. The exercises here show you some quick and clever ways to paint skies.

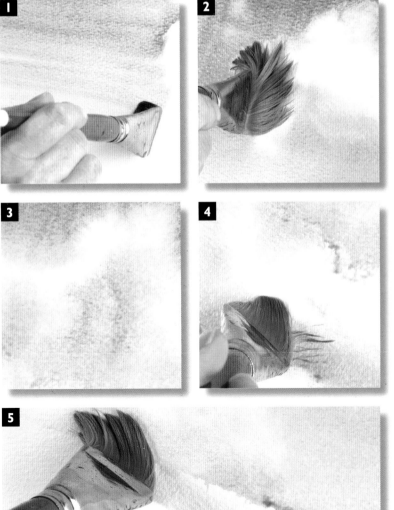

It's important to get this exercise done in less than five minutes – two or three is ideal, as beyond that the paper will start to dry, and taking pigment out of drying paper results in sharp edges.

1 Wet a rectangle of paper with a large flat wash brush, then stroke a watery wash of French ultramarine over the whole piece of paper.
2 Rinse out with water, then squeeze the brush until it's slightly damp, then use it to draw the pigment off the paper to make cloud shapes.
3 For the cloud shadows, drop a very watery mix of French ultramarine and light red into the bases of the clouds.
4 Draw out the pigment as before to soften the edges.
5 Wet the brush with a little clean water and squeeze most of it before mopping out the bottom line. There you go.

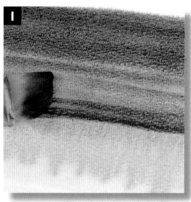

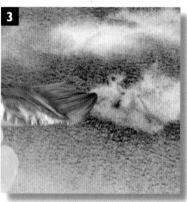

You should run if you see a sky like this! I use a brush to draw out pigment for two reasons: first, it gives a softer edge than can be got from a kitchen roll piece or sponge, and second, it means I don't have to carry lots of extra gear around with me. Using the brush also leaves some of the underlying colour in place.

1 Using a flat wash brush, wet the entire area and stroke yellow ochre across the bottom third of the paper. Follow this with burnt sienna on the middle third and a mix of French ultramarine and burnt sienna from the top, all the way through the other colours, so as to avoid sharp joining lines – the other colours will still shine through. Remember that

the colour when dry will be 50 per cent lighter than when it is applied, so don't worry about going in too dark.

2 Make up another mix of French ultramarine and burnt sienna, with more sienna. Paint this into the sky while the other washes are still wet.

3 Wash and squeeze out the brush, and draw or suck clouds from the wet washes.

EXERCISE **ANGRY SKY**

In a way, a neutral sky is almost more of a challenge than the other types seen in these exercises – nothing is happening here, so you need to get what is there down well on the paper.

1 Using a large flat wash brush, wet the paper with clean water and then put a mix of yellow ochre and alizarin crimson across the bottom of the sky. Next, stroke a mix of French ultramarine and light red from the top of the sky all the way down through the first wash; don't stop when the colours meet, but work over so you can see the reddish wash underneath the second one.

2 As for the other exercises, wash and squeeze out the brush and draw out the pigment at the top, to give an impression of a quiet sky with few clouds.

Here's a tip: in a sunset sky the sun has already gone over the horizon, so you should take the pigment out from underneath the clouds.

1 After wetting the paper, put a stroke of yellow ochre across the bottom and another in the middle. Add some light red – this is a powerful colour, so be careful when you use it.

2 Start painting a mix of French ultramarine and burnt sienna from the top, but leave little bits of underlying colour showing to provide the sunset glow.

3 Add more burnt sienna to the mix to darken it, and put in a few sharp bits of darker cloud.

4 Use a cleaned brush to draw out the cloud shapes.

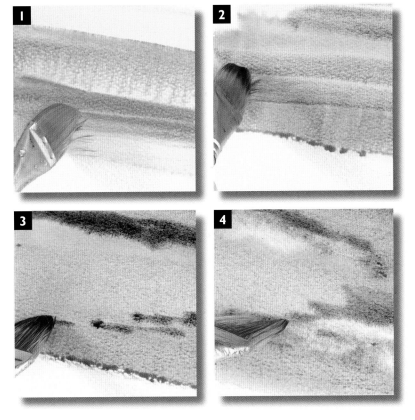

EXERCISE **SUNSET SKY**

Cornfield

This golden view sums up summer in the country – you can almost feel the heat. The project uses just one brush, to keep things as simple as possible.

In addition to using one brush only, I decided not to do any preliminary drawing for this project. The combination fine-tunes your brushstroke skills and you get to find out what your single brush can do. Try to limit yourself to about 10 minutes here, because you have to work quickly to finish.

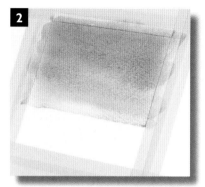

1 Using a ¾ in flat wash brush, I start by wetting the sky area – about two-thirds of the picture – with clean water. I then apply a first wash of watery French ultramarine across the top.

2 I then continue down the paper, using more water and less paint each time. This is known as a graduated wash – but I call it slapping it on quick!

3 After rinsing and squeezing out the brush, I use it to draw out the wet pigment to make cloud shapes.

4 Using clean water, I mop along the bottom edge.

5 While the sky is still very wet, I add a touch of burnt sienna to French ultramarine to make a darker blue, which I then dab into the horizon.

CORNFIELD

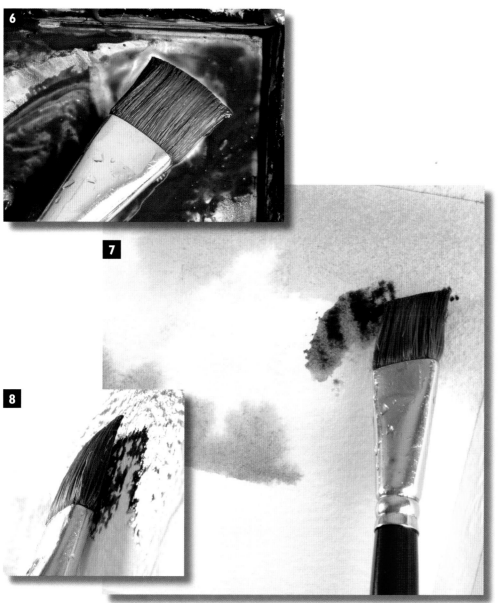

6 For the foliage, I make up a mixture of Hooker's green and burnt sienna, which I keep strong but watery. I dab the brush into the mix, thus loading the hair with lots of paint.

7 To start the foliage for the foreground trees I tap the hair of the brush on to the paper, where it picks up on the rough-textured surface.

8 I make sure the metal of the brush also taps on to the paper – this guarantees that the whole length of the hair is slapping on the paper.

9 The result is a mass of green leaves, but not a solid one, that still has some of the sky colour showing through. As the paint dries, it will show darker and lighter clumps of foliage.

Top Tip

WHEN IT COMES TO PAINTING TREES, UNLESS YOU ARE A BOTANICAL ARTIST, IT'S BEST TO CONCENTRATE ON PAINTING FULL FOLIAGE AS A MASS, NOT ON THE INDIVIDUAL LEAVES.

10 To add liveliness to the foliage, I also use the side of the brush to flick upwards into the greater mass of leaves.

11 I then use the end of the brush hair to create the trunks and large branches. I call this bit 'joining up the dots'.

12 With the brush thoroughly cleaned, I load yellow ochre on to it and make one broad stroke across the paper below the trees, and clean and squeeze out the brush to remove a band at the very bottom – I don't take out too much pigment here, however.

13 This time I squeeze out most of the water and use the end to draw out pigment to make the spaces between the rows of corn.

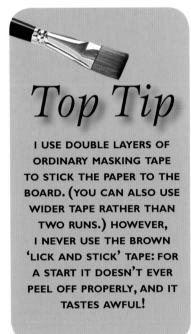

Top Tip

I USE DOUBLE LAYERS OF ORDINARY MASKING TAPE TO STICK THE PAPER TO THE BOARD. (YOU CAN ALSO USE WIDER TAPE RATHER THAN TWO RUNS.) HOWEVER, I NEVER USE THE BROWN 'LICK AND STICK' TAPE: FOR A START IT DOESN'T EVER PEEL OFF PROPERLY, AND IT TASTES AWFUL!

CORNFIELD

14 As I add the lighter rows, I squeeze out the brush every few strokes to make sure I remove the pigment, not just move the paint about.

15 Now I make up a light green from Hooker's green and burnt sienna, and add a few flicks of this into the very foreground.

16 When I push the brush upwards the hairs split apart to give me some blades of grass. I peel off the tape, and there's my picture – not bad!

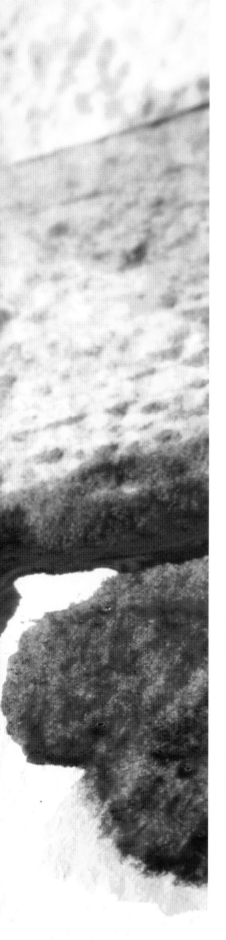

EXERCISE
BOATS AND ROCKS

Although you can sometimes get away with a straight view of the sea, with no other features, there will undoubtedly be times when a bit more interest is needed. Here's how.

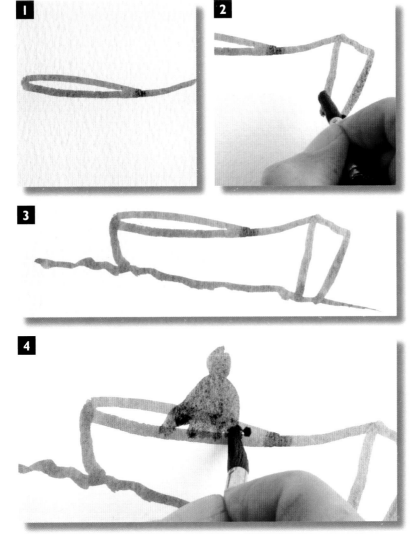

W hat worries many people is painting the front end – the pointed shape – so they tend to put the boat sideways on. If you use a 'fish shape', it becomes easy to make a basic boat.

1 Paint most of the shape of a thin fish, but don't finish the lower tail line.

2 At the end, make an irregular rectangle without the bottom line that closes the box.

3 A light, squiggly line to make the sea, and you have an effective simple boat.

4 One round blob for the head, an elongated one for the body and another one for the arm and even an oar, and there's your rowing boat.

1

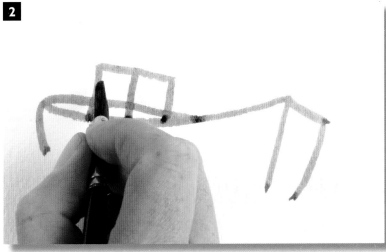

2

Once you get used to working with the fish shape to start your boats, you can then expand your repertoire with just a few simple strokes of the brush. Here's a fishing trawler to give you an idea.

1 With one flowing brushstroke, paint the fish shape, this time bringing the 'tail' up and then down at the end corner.
2 Stick a box on top, making sure that the box corners are correct for the angle at which the boat is to your view. Add a couple of simple strokes for windows, block in the box side, then put in a couple of masts and a lapping sea line, and that's the trawler done.

EXERCISE TRAWLER

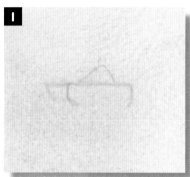

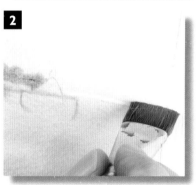

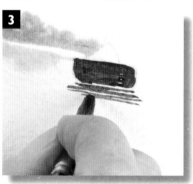

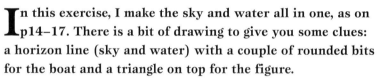

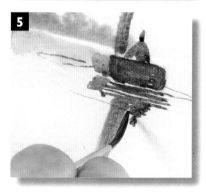

I n this exercise, I make the sky and water all in one, as on p14–17. There is a bit of drawing to give you some clues: a horizon line (sky and water) with a couple of rounded bits for the boat and a triangle on top for the figure.

1 Wet all the paper, and wash light red across the middle, and a mix of French ultramarine and light red at top and bottom. Draw out the clouds and leave to dry a bit.

2 Drop in a darker version of the mix, stopping at the boat, then draw out a separation line in the middle of the picture and leave to dry fully.

3 Use a fairly strong mix of raw umber and burnt sienna to make burnt umber for the side

of the boat, and a lighter version for the sides and reflection, which is in strands, not solid.

4 For the sail, use light red, and repeat underneath lighter for the reflection.

5 Add the shadow-side of the sail in a mix of French ultramarine and burnt sienna, darker than the trees, and use the same mix for the reflection and the figure in the boat. Finish with a few ripples.

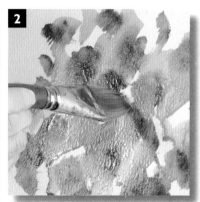

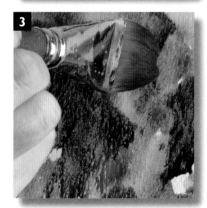

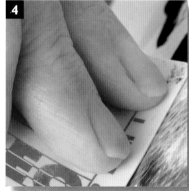

You can go into detail when painting rocks, but this takes up a lot of time. My way uses few colours and a credit card – if you want smaller rocks, cut up the card, which will save you money as well!

1 Use a flat wash brush to dab on light marks of yellow ochre.
2 Wash the brush and, while the ochre is wet, add mid-tone colours using raw umber.
3 Make a black from French ultramarine and burnt sienna and add this, leaving some patches of white on the paper.
4 Scrape the credit card over the wet paint to create a clump of individual rocks; don't be loose with the card, but dig it in. And there are your rocks!

C. M. EVANS. 04

Seascape

The combination of open sea and big sky is an
irresistible one. You don't need to work on details
here, but can concentrate on getting the mood.

Some of the best beaches in the world, in my opinion, are in Northumberland where I live: beautiful and uncluttered. Even if it's a bit cold and windy, a day where the light is not too bright is perfect for painting, as you can see what you're doing – on a glorious sunny day, you can't see anything for the brilliant white paper.

1 The most important line is the sea line: this doesn't have to be perfectly straight, but it mustn't be wobbly. To get a straight line, I draw against another piece of paper – no problem!

2 I use seawater to wet the sky area with a 1½ in wash brush, and then apply a wash of alizarin crimson and yellow ochre at the base, then French ultramarine above, blending the paint together.

3 After washing out the brush and squeezing out the water, I use it to suck out the paint along the

SEASCAPE

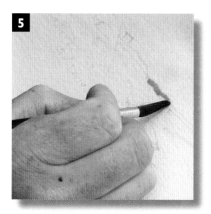

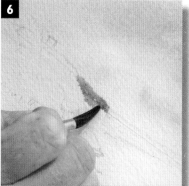

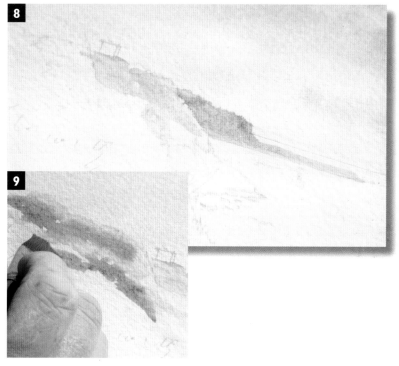

bottom line and take off the paint for the clouds. The idea here is to work fast before the paint dries, and to sum up the feel of the sky, not chase the clouds – they'll always win.

4 In the sky I drop in some French ultramarine mixed with a little light red for more clouds, then rinse and squeeze the brush again and use it to take out the excess at the bottom. I now let the painting dry; any flies that get stuck to it can become birds in the picture later.

5 When everything is completely dry, I start on the sand dunes on the distant headland, putting on a mix of French ultramarine and light red very loosely with a No. 8 round brush.

6 While this wash is still wet, I add a tiny bit of yellow ochre below it.

7 I clean the brush in water, squeeze it until it's just a bit damp and quickly merge the two washes together to create a nice soft edge.

8 I put in a weakish wash of yellow ochre for the next hill on the left.

9 While this wash is still wet, I drop in a mix of Hooker's green and yellow ochre so that the colours merge, leaving no hard edges. I then add slightly weaker mixes further into the distance.

10 I use French ultramarine with a tiny bit of light red for the distant building – which is an old coastal defence bunker – putting more water into the mix for the side edge and making it darker in the shadows. I then let everything dry completely.

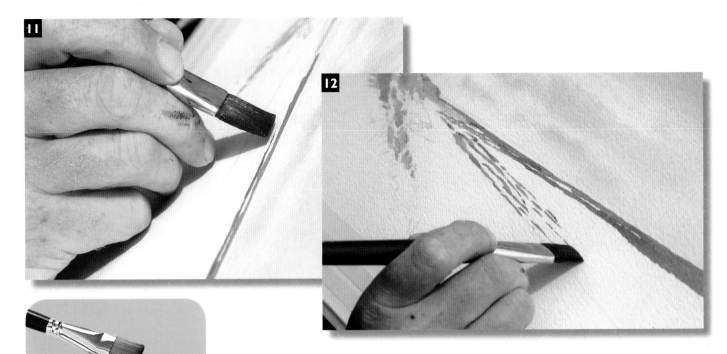

Top Tip

WHENEVER YOU NEED TO LET WASHES DRY BEFORE CONTINUING, USE THE TIME TO CHANGE THE SEAWATER IN YOUR BUCKET – THE WALK WILL DO YOU GOOD, AND YOU CAN COME BACK TO LOOK AT THE PAINTING AGAIN WITH A FRESH EYE.

11 Now it's time to start the sea, using my Charles Evans British sea colour – this can be used as a base colour for mixes, but today I'm using it as it comes. Switching back to the ¾in wash brush, I start with the horizon line.

12 As I get nearer to the the headland and beach, I just tap the brush on to the paper, then add a few squiggly lines the closer I get to shore. At this stage I leave a lot of white paper between the brush marks for highlights.

13 As before, I wash and squeeze out the brush to pull out paint for the ripples in the waves, and let the painting dry again.

SEASCAPE

14 With everything dry, I make up a mix of the Charles Evans sand colour – this is also a useful colour for lightening mixes, while not being opaque like white paint. This time I use it as a base colour, adding a little French ultramarine and a lot of water, then make wide strokes to block in the basic colour of the sand. (On warmer beaches, I might use tiny amounts of yellow ochre or burnt sienna.)

15 After taking the sand just into the sea areas, I bring a darker, but still watery, wash of the sea colour over the sand. I then reinforce the very light sea washes, still leaving plenty of white highlights on the paper.

16 Switching to the No. 8 round brush, I mix the sand colour with some raw umber for the stones in the middle distance – I'm not trying to paint every single one, but to give an impression of the lines and shapes of the stones.

17 I use a mix of French ultramarine with a little light red and plenty of water to paint some dips and gullies in the sand dunes among the grasses. As in any painting, these darker touches make the most of the lighter areas around them.

18 For the smaller touches on the beach – the darker patches of sand, strands of seaweed, stones and pebbles – I use a darkish mix of French ultramarine and burnt sienna.

Seascape **41**

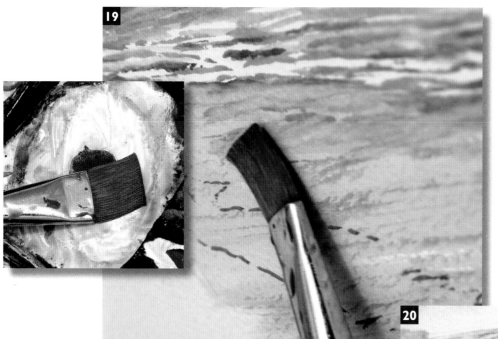

19 Using the same mix as for step 18, only this time going back to the ¾ in flat wash brush, I lightly brush over the surface of the paper to create a sparkling texture on the sand.
20 Switching back to the No. 8 round brush, I then add some more dark areas in the sea and along the shore line.

21 I now make up a warmish mix of the Charles Evans sea colour and yellow ochre, and paint this into the nearest sand dunes with the ¾ in flat brush. I flick the brush up to go into the darkest areas here, and then use a mix of Hooker's green and yellow ochre in the same area – again, I flick up into the yellow for tall, windswept grasses, being careful to leave white highlights.
22 In the foreground I paint on a mix of Hooker's green and burnt sienna – because the colours will dry up to 50 per cent lighter than when applied, I use quite a strong mix.

SEASCAPE

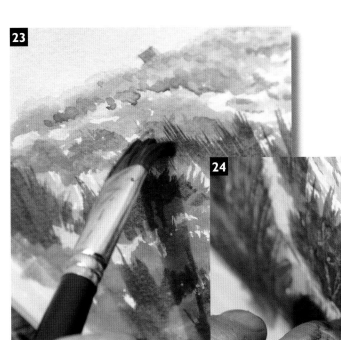

23 I now make up a mix of French ultramarine and light red with lots of water, and use this to go even darker on to the dune grasses in the foreground. As well as the flat of the bristles, I use the side of the brush to get the effects I want – it's worth experimenting with all angles and all parts of the brush to see what you can do.

24 While the wash is still wet. I scratch into the paint with my fingernails to give the impression of light and stalks without trying to get in every single one.

25 Using the mixture from step 23, I switch to a No. 3 rigger brush to put a few seagulls in the sky and a few vertical marks in the far distance, making sure that these are smaller the further away they are. I finish by taking off the tape – and there's the painting!

EXERCISE
TREES IN WATERCOLOUR

It's almost traditional for trees to cause all sorts of problems, but the following pages show you how to get quick and clever results with watercolour paints.

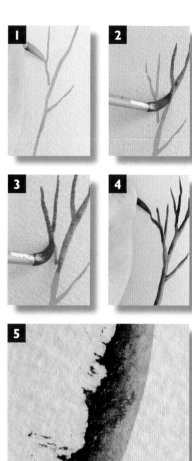

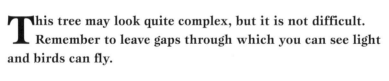

This tree may look quite complex, but it is not difficult. Remember to leave gaps through which you can see light and birds can fly.

1 Using a No. 8 round brush, make simple outlines of trunk and branches in yellow ochre.
2 While this is wet, with the same brush put raw umber on the shadow side, opposite to where the light is coming from.
3 The colours run into one another, so there are no hard edges where they meet. This gives a rounded effect.
4 Add a mix of burnt sienna and French ultramarine for a few twigs.

5 To create the impression of rough growth, flick out from the trunk with a No. 3 rigger brush and using the same mix, which adds detail.
6 Now for the canopy of foliage. take up yellow ochre with a ¾ in wash brush, and tap it on from the brush side, then do the same with a mix of Hooker's green and burnt sienna.
7 For the shadow areas, tap on a mix of burnt sienna and French ultramarine blue.

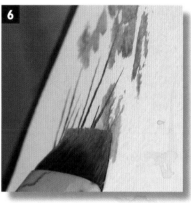

Even though there is hardly any foliage here, the temptation is just the same as for trees with a canopy of leaves: to paint more than you actually need to.

1 Using the No. 8 round brush, make a simple outline of the main trunk and boughs with a mix of French ultramarine blue and burnt sienna.

2 Switching to a No. 3 rigger brush, add a bit of rough on the side by holding the full length of the brush head against the trunk and flicking out. The surface of the paper catches some of the paint and creates a drybrush effect.

3 This time using the tip of the rigger brush and the same wash, add a few twigs – don't go mad trying to add thousands of twigs, but keep it simple.

4 It's again much better to create an impression of a little winter foliage, so take the French ultramarine blue and burnt sienna mix on the ¾ in wash brush and very lightly tap this. And there you are – a stark winter tree!

EXERCISE WINTER TREE

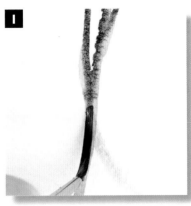

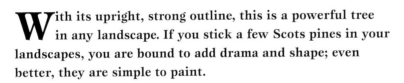

With its upright, strong outline, this is a powerful tree in any landscape. If you stick a few Scots pines in your landscapes, you are bound to add drama and shape; even better, they are simple to paint.

1 Take some yellow ochre with a No. 3 rigger brush and paint the trunk of a tall, slim tree – you can add as many boughs as you like, so long as the trunk shape isn't changed. While the first wash is wet, paint a mix of French ultramarine and burnt sienna down the side of the tree opposite the light.

2 Now for a technical term: use the second mix to add some squiggly bits on top, then move down the tree.

3 Next switch to a ¾ in wash brush and load this with yellow ochre. Add dabs with the flat bristles for the foliage.

4 While this wash is still wet, make a mix of Hooker's green, burnt sienna and French ultramarine, and add a dollop of this among the yellow ochre. Continue steps for the foliage further down the tree, and finish by putting in a few dabs and upstrokes of the green mix for the grass at the trunk base.

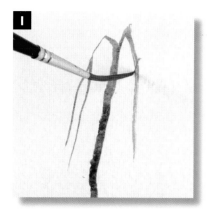

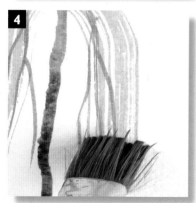

Weeping willows are lovely, atmospheric trees that really enhance a landscape. They have the reputation of being difficult to paint effectively, but here's how to achieve good results quickly.

1 Starting with a wash of raw umber, pull a No. 3 rigger brush up the paper for the main trunk, and then at the top turn the brush upside down and bring it back again for the 'weeping' branches. Repeat this routine, each time slightly thickening the trunk and adding another branch.

2 Good brushes are strong and will take any amount of abuse. So, once you've made a mix of Hooker's green and yellow ochre, split a ¾in wash brush by bashing its head into the palette.

3 Push the split bristles into the paint.

4 Starting from the top of the tree, drag the brush down in sweeping curves. Add a little ground at the base, and there is a weeping willow.

Overgrown and dead trees can be tricky, as you have to suggest the underlying shape of the trunk and branches without showing them. Try this method.

1 As for the willow on the previous pages, start by splitting a No. 8 round brush and then take yellow ochre from the palette.
2 Stipple on the colour in the rough shape of the trunk and main branches, making sure to leave white highlights of paper showing through.
3 Now make up a mix of Hooker's green and burnt

sienna, and repeat the stippling, leaving some of the first colour to show the lighter side. Mix French ultramarine and burnt sienna, and repeat to darken further.
4 For the twigs, use a No. 3 rigger brush, and make a mix of raw umber and burnt sienna for the branches at the top. A final splash of green anchors the tree to the ground.

This particular species has a reputation of being notoriously difficult to paint. It's not the shape of the foliage that's tricky – it's the ridges and knobbly bits on the central trunk. But fear not; it can be done.

1 Using a No. 8 round brush, paint the trunk with a mix of yellow ochre and raw umber and let it dry; but you can use any colour you like, as it's just so as not to have white paper.
2 For the important strokes, make a mix of French ultramarine and burnt sienna, and applied it thus: hold the brush upright – not like a pencil – with the full length of the hairs resting on the paper, and drag it across the first wash, starting at the bottom and working up with less paint.
3 To finish add a few branches with a slightly darker version of the second mix.

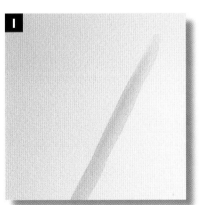

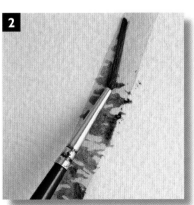

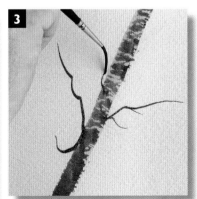

EXERCISE **SILVER BIRCH**

Landscape With People

*The still trees and calm water give a tranquil feel
to this view. But there's a storm brewing, just look
at that cloud shadow in the foreground.*

After masking the picture area, I make a simple outline drawing: first a squiggly line for the middle-distance trees, then a bank coming down on one side, out of the picture area. Next, the path comes in from the middle distance – here, the key thing is to make sure it is wider in the foreground. I add a few sticks to indicate the most prominent trees, followed by the water line and the bank on the far side of the river, and then I complete the drawing with a couple of poplars on the left-hand bank.

1

1 I wet the whole sky area with lots of water, then use a mix of alizarin crimson and yellow ochre, again watery, in the bottom third of the sky, all applied with a 1½ in wash brush.

2

3

4

5

6

2 Using plenty of colour and a 1½ in wash brush, I paint a mix of French ultramarine and light red right through the other washes down to the bottom of the sky area.
3 I finish this part by using an almost dry brush to mop up the bottom line, and then squeeze out the brush and suck out the clouds.
4 To get a hazy, distant feel to the trees in the middle distance, I use the ¾ in wash brush to dab yellow ochre, followed quickly by a mix of Hooker's green and burnt sienna, using the side of the brush.
5 I make a nasty purple with French ultramarine and alizarin crimson, then knock this 'chameleon' colour back with burnt sienna, and paint over the trees.
6 I mop up along the bottom of the trees to make a sharp line.

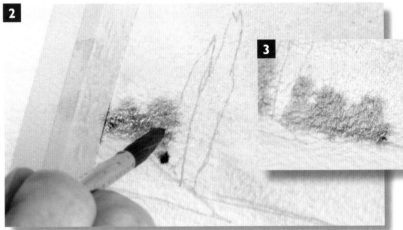

7 With the tree washes in place and still wet, I squeeze the ¾in wash brush firmly between my fingers to dry it out.

8 One of the myths of water-colour is that once you've made a mark you can't undo or change it. Rather than painting around the closer tree shapes, I simply use the dried wash brush to suck out the wet paint where the trees need to go.

9 For the poplars on the left, I put a daub of yellow ochre on each tree, and follow this up by splashing on a mix of Hooker's green and yellow ochre.

10 I then add a touch of my shadow mix – French ultramarine and alizarin crimson – to the left-hand side of each poplar to finish these trees.

11 Next I repeat the same mixes in the same order for the bank between the poplars and the water; and that side of the picture is now complete.

12 Going back to the trees on the right side, I paint them in with yellow ochre using my No. 3 rigger brush, as I showed you in the tips and techniques on pages 46–51.

13 Using the same brush, I add raw umber to the left of the yellow ochre.

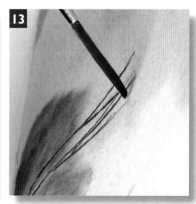

14 I next use the rigger brush to add the mix of French ultramarine and burnt sienna to the left of the raw umber, and then let the colours dry.

15 With the top edge of the ¾in wash brush, I start the foliage with dabs of yellow ochre.

16 While this first wash is still wet, I dab on a mixture of Hooker's green and burnt sienna, and then add the shadow mix among the foliage.

17 I load yellow ochre on to the same brush and use this to make the bank in front of the right-hand trees, and then add a mix of Hooker's green and burnt sienna below that to make it look as if the trees are standing on something. The next stage is to let all this dry.

That's the top half of the picture complete. Now I'm going to treat the water very much like the sky wash, and I expect to finish it in a few minutes, while the paper is sopping wet. I'm not intending to attempt perfect reflections, but to echo and capture the colours of the land features in the water. Usually, it's a good idea to make the reflection darker than the object itself.

18 First, I put lots of water into the water area, then drop a nice dark mix of Hooker's green and burnt sienna under the trees in the middle distance, using the ¾in wash brush, then put some of this mix under the poplars on the right.

19 I then drop a touch of French ultramarine into some of the green reflected areas.

20 A touch of green mix goes nicely under the poplars.

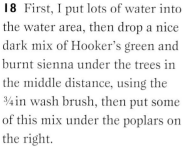

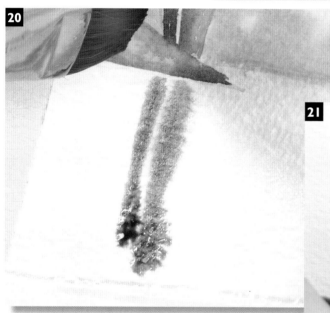

21 A touch of yellow ochre sits next to the green mix to show the reflection of the lighter side of the poplars.

22 Using a mix of French ultramarine with a tiny amount of light red, I fill in the middle parts of the water. Although I am moving the paint around on the wet paper, I make sure to go in one direction only – going in with the pigment and dragging out the ready-painted reflections only muddies the colours.

23 I mix the colours in the water by stroking the blue mix over the reflections.

24 Before the washes dry, I rinse, squeeze and shape the bristles of the brush and use it to draw out the pigment along to the right of the water area. Again, this effect can be spoilt if it's overdone, so I aim for just a few horizontal lines of highlighted white paper.

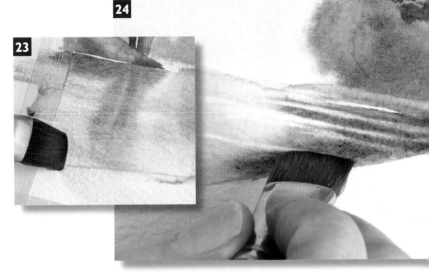

25 Having decided I want to add a couple of people to the picture, even though the right-hand trees are dry, I use clean water to dabble a wet round brush to suck out the paint and reveal lighter areas where I will place the people.

26 I put washes of yellow ochre on the path, lighter in the distance and a little stronger in the foreground, and then use the tip of the wash brush to show the rounded contours of the ground on the left, using a little raw umber mixed into the yellow ochre.

27 Sticking to the ¾ in wash brush, I repeat this for the ground to the right of the path.

LANDSCAPE WITH PEOPLE

28 For the grass by the water's edge I use the wash brush to slap on a mix of Hooker's green, yellow ochre and a touch of French ultramarine, plus plenty of water; I'm not after much detail.

29 I break up the edge of the path with a few flicks of the green mix, using the ¾in wash brush for the ground contours; again, I avoid putting in too much detail.

30 To add patches of grass to the centre of the path, I rock the wash brush backwards and forwards, creating a rough effect.

31 While the green dries, I go back to the people with the rigger brush. I place a couple of blobs of a mix of yellow ochre and alizarin crimson for the heads, add some alizarin crimson for one top, then a mixture of French ultramarine and burnt sienna for the legs – and the blobs become people.

32 Now I do something really scary: I mix French ultramarine and alizarin crimson, knocking it back with a bit of burnt sienna and plenty of water, and then pull big strokes of this over the whole foreground area with the wash brush.

33 I finish by inventing shadows for the people, plus one for a thin tree, and then add some dark tones within the dark areas to establish the edge of the path. That's it; all done.

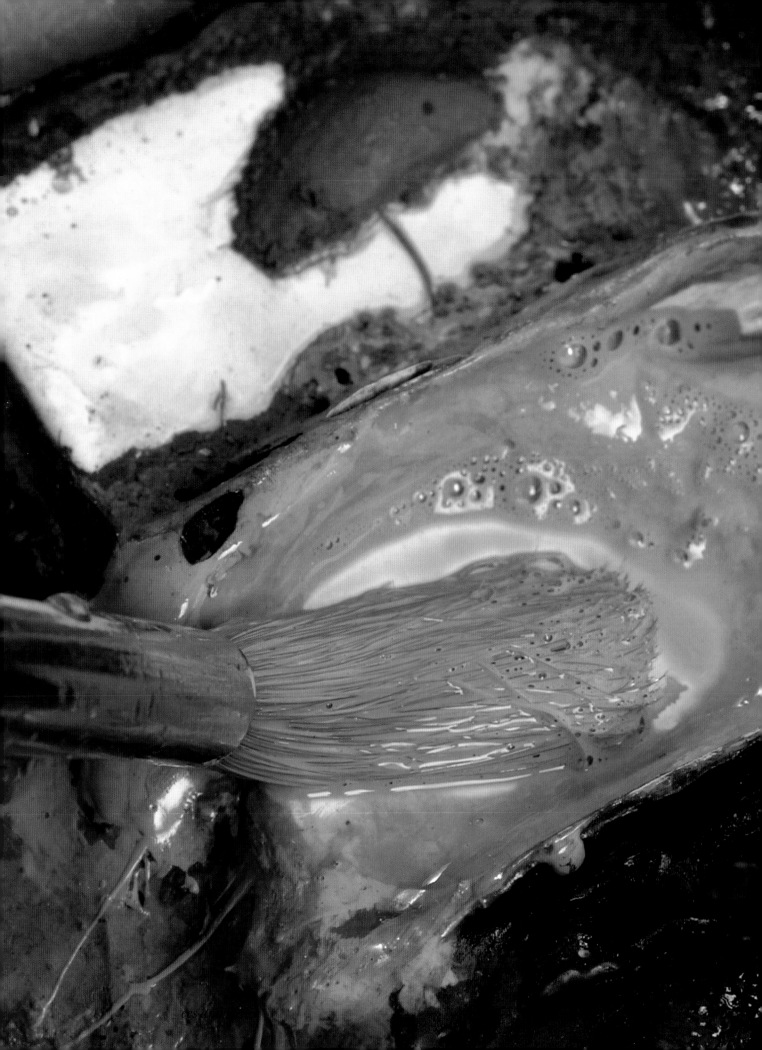

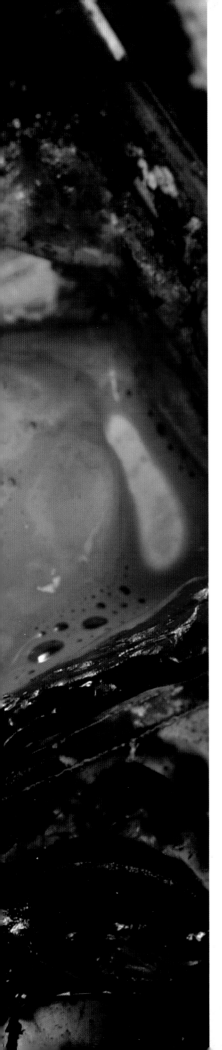

EXERCISE
PEOPLE AND ANIMALS

Don't worry – 'people' here doesn't mean life drawing! Keep people and animals small and in the middle distance, and make your people walk away from you, and you should be fine.

There are lots of methods used to paint people, but I reckon that if you can paint a 'Y' and a 'P', you shouldn't have any problems with painting people. As a free gift, here's a dog as well.

1 Using a small round brush and any colour you like, put two full stops on the paper. Leave a little gap below the stop on the right, switch colours and add 'P'.
2 After filling in the empty part of the 'P', change colours again and paint a reversed 'P' under the left-hand stop, once more leaving a tiny gap.
3 Fill in the second body and then change colours and draw the letter 'Y' under the first figure, this time joining it up to the bottom of the body.
4 When filling this in, leave a tiny bit of white paper to suggest the gap between the thighs. Paint the next 'Y' and fill it in, before making a few strokes to show the ground.
5 For the dog paint a square and a smaller square on top on the right.
6 Then add two sticks joined on to the larger square below and one above, and there you are – done!

EXERCISE **COUPLE AND DOG**

For sheep, you don't need to see four legs, two ears and a wagging tail – all you need is a loaf of bread with a lump on the end! Here's what I mean.

1 Start by drawing the loaf and the lump at one end, with a bit sticking out of the lump for an ear. Note that you don't even need to draw the lines right down to the ground.

2 Using a No. 8 round brush, put a few dabs of yellow ochre along the top of the loaf, going up to the drawn edge. Then put a mix of French ultramarine and burnt sienna at the right end of the loaf and a line to make an incomplete 'V' below.

3 Using the same mix, colour in part of the bottom of the loaf.

4 Now add a few dabs of the second mix to the yellow at the top and switch to a dry brush to mix the two washes together.

5 After mixing the French ultramarine and burnt sienna to a black, colour in the lump at the end of the loaf. A few strokes of green for grass, and there's the sheep grazing away contentedly.

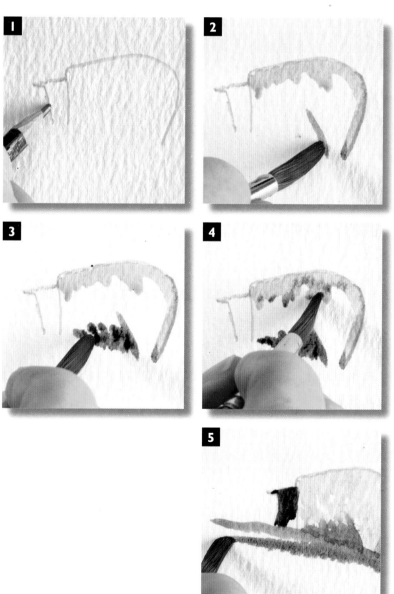

As with all the animals here, you need to make them small and put them in the middle distance or even further away – we're not talking about the cover of a farming magazine!

1 Start by mixing a light wash of French ultramarine and burnt sienna to make a grey, and then use a No. 8 round brush to paint a series of triangles as shown. Don't forget the tail, which hangs off the back triangle.
2 With a black mix of the same colours, colour in parts of the triangles in cow markings. Then it's just a matter of sticking an ear on and some dangly bits underneath, a line to represent the ground, and there's your cow.

Traditionally, horses are among the most difficult things to paint, because they are complex. But if your horse is in the middle distance, all you need is a light bulb.

1 Making up your horse colour from raw umber, paint a thin light bulb and add two sticks off the top and a block at the end of them to make the head.

2 With the same mix colour the horse, leaving a little white paper as a highlight.

3 Then use a darker version of the mix for the mane, tail and shadows, then rinse and squeeze out the brush to take off paint for contours. If you want the horse to be grazing, simply angle the sticks and head of step 1 downwards (as shown above).

Cows and Sheep

A pastoral scene with grazing animals is always attractive – and cows and sheep usually stay still long enough for you to paint them!

ompared to the finished painting shown on the previous pages, the initial drawing here may look a bit bare and lacking in detail – but that's all part of the plan. If you aren't completely bound by pencil lines, you have more freedom to use techniques such as blending and softening, drawing out paint and so on.

1 After masking the edges of the paper, I make the inital drawing as a guide to get me started. I then apply a very well watered-down wash of yellow ochre, using a ¾in wash brush, over everything...

2 ...with the exception of the shapes of the cows and sheep. I'm not using masking fluid for this because there is nothing else happening, so it is easy.

3 I allow the first wash to dry, then use a mix of cobalt blue and plenty of water to block in the sky, this time leaving the cloud areas unpainted. I also soften the bits where the blue meets the unpainted areas.

4 With a mix of cobalt blue and light red I drop in a few cloud shadows using the side of the brush, and allow all this to dry for a while.

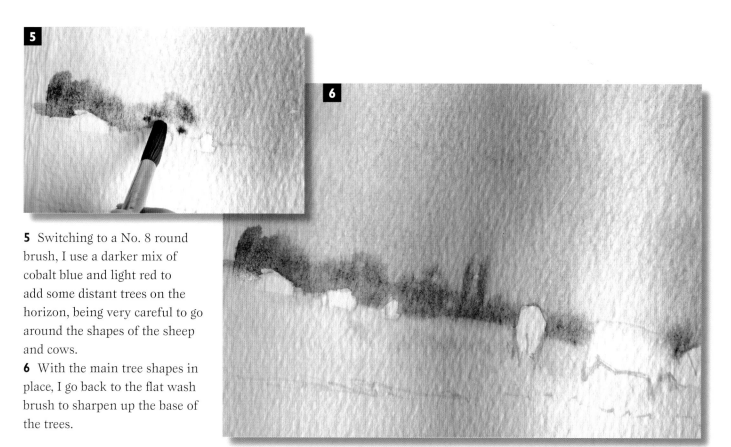

5 Switching to a No. 8 round brush, I use a darker mix of cobalt blue and light red to add some distant trees on the horizon, being very careful to go around the shapes of the sheep and cows.

6 With the main tree shapes in place, I go back to the flat wash brush to sharpen up the base of the trees.

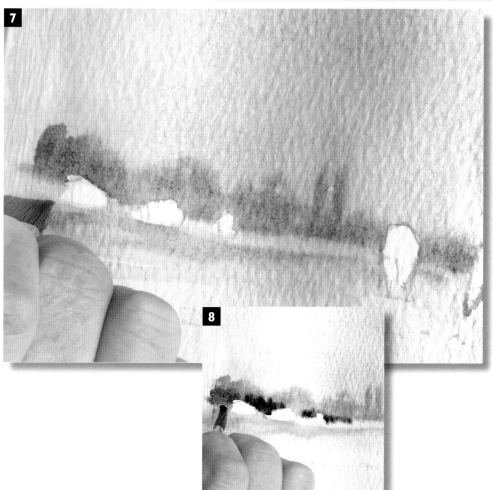

7 I now use the flat brush to drop in a light wash of light red across the ground in the middle distance, allowing the original wash of yellow ochre below to show through.

8 While this wash is drying, I switch back to the No. 8 round brush and use a quite dark mix of cobalt blue and light red for the darkest trees on the far left of the picture. Here, my aim is to have a dark enough area to accentuate the white patches that are the sheep.

9 I make up a black with a mix of French ultramarine and burnt sienna, and drop this as a first touch of colour on what will become the main cow in the picture. While this is drying, I make up a mix of raw umber and light red, and use this to add colour and shape to the cows on either side.

10 After mixing Hooker's green and burnt sienna with plenty of water to make a nice watery green, I switch to a No. 3 rigger brush for the leaves on the right-hand foreground tree. I use the brush on its side to create bunches of leaves, and make sure not to carry surplus water on the brush, which could run and make too large a mark.

Top Tip

KEEP LOOKING OVER THE WHOLE PICTURE REGULARLY – STANDING BACK HELPS. EVEN WHEN YOU'VE DECIDED TO WORK QUICKLY, TAKING FREQUENT OVERVIEWS CAN BE INVALUABLE.

COWS AND SHEEP

11 With a mix of cobalt blue and light red I use the tip of the rigger brush to make branches that link the green splodges of leaves.

12 I wash and almost completely dry the brush, and then use it to add tiny touches of shadow colour created with a mix of burnt sienna and French ultramarine – nowhere near as strong or dark as the mix I made with the same colours for step 9.

13 However, I do use the black mix of burnt sienna and French ultramarine for small blobs that I shape to make the heads of the distant sheep.

14 Still using the rigger brush, I add a touch of yellow ochre on to their backs. I let this dry a bit and then put a tiny touch of a light mix of French ultramarine and burnt sienna for the shadows.

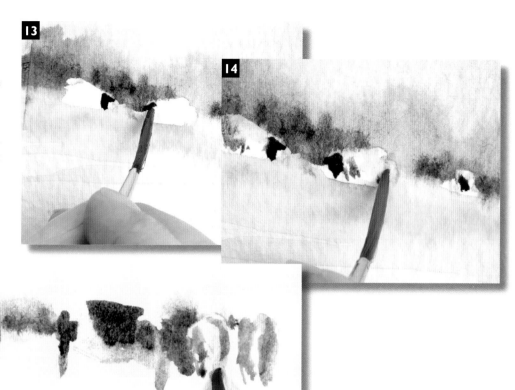

15 With the same shadow mix, but after watering it down to make a very weak mix, I go back to the cows; to capture light on the top and on parts of the sides, I leave some areas unpainted.

16 I make a mix of light red and burnt sienna and use the No. 8 round brush to add a few marks and flicks on either side of the main right-hand tree.

17 Sticking with the same brush, I make up a sepia from burnt umber and French ultramarine and make a few more flicks upwards underneath the tree. I use the same combination to create small branches and twigs at the side of the trunk.

18 For the foreground I go back to the flat brush to lightly stroke a watery mix of yellow ochre and raw umber over the area, leaving sparkles of white paper showing through.

19 I now mix Hooker's green and light red, and put just a bit of pigment on the tip, dabbing this colour on to create the idea of rough grass.

20 Here and there I flick the brush upwards to join the colour to the dark undergrowth at the base of the tree.

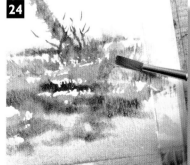

21 I take the same colour over to the middle of the picture and paint a band of grass around and to the right of the group of cows.

22 Using my 'shadow mixture' of French ultramarine, alizarin crimson and burnt sienna, I add some shadow detail underneath the cows with the No. 8 round brush.

23 I use the same mix and brush to add just a few shadows to the foreground grasses...

24 ...and some more touches to the sides of the path; these also help to create contours and show the bumpy nature of the ground.

COWS AND SHEEP

25 I think this picture needs a few verticals in it, to add a sense of depth and recession, and to help make the whole thing feel more complete. So I make up a mix of raw umber, burnt sienna and French ultramarine, and use the rigger brush to add some old wooden fence posts.

26 Any kind of vertical is a great aid to creating depth and distance. I make sure that the posts get smaller as they go away from the foreground, and join them up with irregular horizontal strokes – a brand-new, uniform fence would distract the eye from the main focal points and make the painting look regimented.

27 It's all nearly done now. When everything is dry, I take a good look at the whole painting and make the decisions for the finishing touches. Here I go back to the darkest black mix of French ultramarine and burnt sienna and put in a very few darker markings on the black and white cow.

28 With the darkest markings in place, I just reinforce some of the shadows beneath the cows – and that's it!

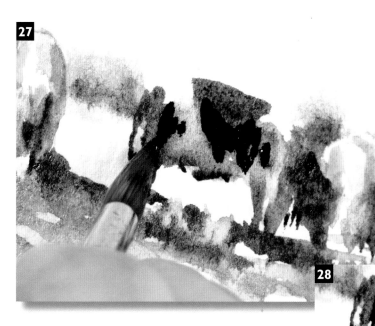

EXERCISE
TREES IN WATERCOLOUR PENCIL

The next project (see page 81) uses watercolour pencils as a variation on paints; try out the trees in these exercises to give you a feel for using these versatile tools.

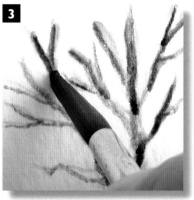

When painting bare winter trees, I always exaggerate their darkness to make the overall result more effective, especially on a lone tree as shown here.

1 Draw the basic shape of the trunk and main branches with a black watercolour pencil; don't try to make the colour too dark when drawing.

2 Next put yellow ochre pencil on one side of the tree and along most of the branches. Don't try to follow the exact line of the black, but give the impression of a canopy of twigs.

3 Taking clean water on a No. 8 round brush, go over the whole tree. This darkens the colours and gives a varied texture – you don't want to smoothe everything out.

4 Rinsing the brush, take up just a little heavily watered black pencil to show the winter growth and ground – and there you have it!

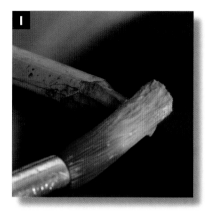

For a tree in full foliage, try mixing all the colours on the brush – just as you'd do for watercolour paints, only taking the pigment from the point of the pencil.

1 First dip a No. 8 round brush in clean water, make a mixture of dark green and brown ochre from the watercolour pencils.
2 Then dab the brush on the paper to make masses of leaves – keep everything light at this stage, and don't worry about little dots of accumulated pigment here and there.

3 While the paint is still wet, quickly add some blue-grey to the mix on the brush and again dab this on for the darker parts of the foliage, still leaving white paper for birds to fly through.
4 To finish, clean the brush, take straight blue-grey on to it from the pencil, and drag the pigment for the branches, trunk and ground at the base.

EXERCISE TREE IN LEAF

1 The first pencil colour is brown ochre, which you can use for the lightest tones on the tree.
2 Follow this on one side with brown pencil – don't try to cover all the paper with the pencil marks, as the water will do that later.
3 Next add some black pencil for the darkest, shadowed side.
4 At the moment everything looks like a vertically striped, odd-coloured stick of rock with a growth on the side...
5 ... but dip a No. 8 round brush in clean water and stroke the tip on to the pencil marks...
6 ... blending the colours as you go. It's important to just make the strokes along the length of the trunk – if you mess about too much and go back over what you've done with the brush, the effect will be muddy.
7 Drag some of the merged colour from the trunk to make a few branches and twigs.
8 After rinsing the brush go gently along the main branch, again being careful not to overblend or merge the colours.
9 Let everything dry, and hey presto! you have a lovely rounded tree trunk with knots and all.

This exercise uses both dry watercolour pencil work and brushwork to give a strong final effect. The main things here are to work quickly when adding the water to the pigment marks and not to spend time looking for a polished result – the roughness makes the character of this tree.

EXERCISE **BLENDING TREES**

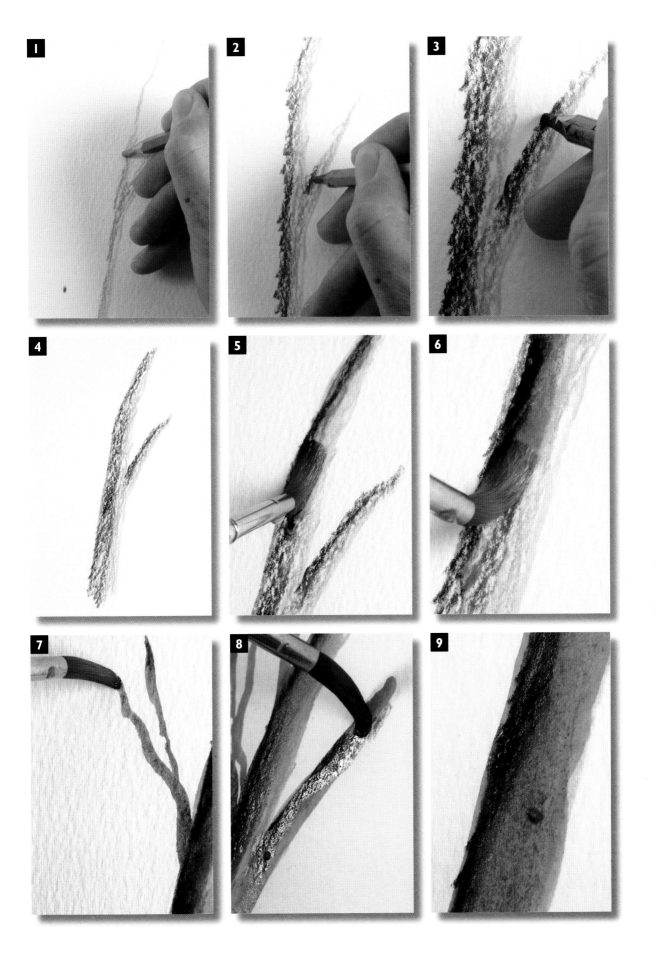

EXERCISE **BLENDING TREES**

Water Scene

This peaceful little scene is very quick and easy to

do: all you need is a box of watercolour pencils,

a brush, some water and a pen to finish off.

I have owned my tin of 24 Derwent watercolour pencils for over six years now, and I am still using all the original pencils – so this is a pretty economical way to work! (It also helps that I use a sharp knife for sharpening, not a pencil sharpener, which eats any pencil quickly.) As usual, for this project I start with gunmetal grey for the very simple outline; unlike a standard pencil, with watercolour pencil the lines disappear when water is applied, so all I am doing at this point is providing a few guiding lines.

1

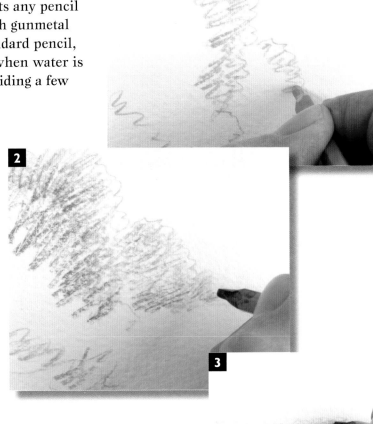

2

3

1 Inside the tree outlines, I add a little bit of brown ochre, just colouring in like a child's drawing and capturing light here and there by leaving patches of white paper.
2 Now I continue this colouring in with dark green, going over the ochre in places.
3 With watercolour pencils, the harder they are pressed, the stronger the colour they provide, so I get a feeling of recession by lightening the pressure as I go.

WATER SCENE

4 Moving on to the distant bank, I put in a tiny touch of purple, using nice light strokes above a very sparse line of brown ochre. I'm making no attempt to keep the lines straight, but looking for bumps.

5 Going back to the first area, I put blue-grey marks across the other colours.

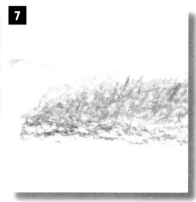

6 With watercolour paints, I use Hooker's green; with watercolour pencils, I put the colours on top of each other – first the blue...

7 ... and then the yellow. It may not be green yet, but just hang on.

8 Right – that's the main bit of drawing done. Now it's time for the magic!

9 For a large area of one colour, scratching and then wetting pencil lines doesn't give a very smooth result, so with a No. 8 round brush and clean water, I stroke Prussian blue off the pencil and start to make washes for the sky. Some people call this a graduated wash – I say whack it on!

10 Now I rinse the brush and stroke some blue-grey off the pencil to add clouds; and there's a quick and clever way to make a watercolour pencil sky.

11 For the rest of the painting where there are pencil marks, I simply go over the marks with a clean brush and merge the colours together.

12 With every stroke of the brush, I'm creating new colours and blends as the water merges the colours together.

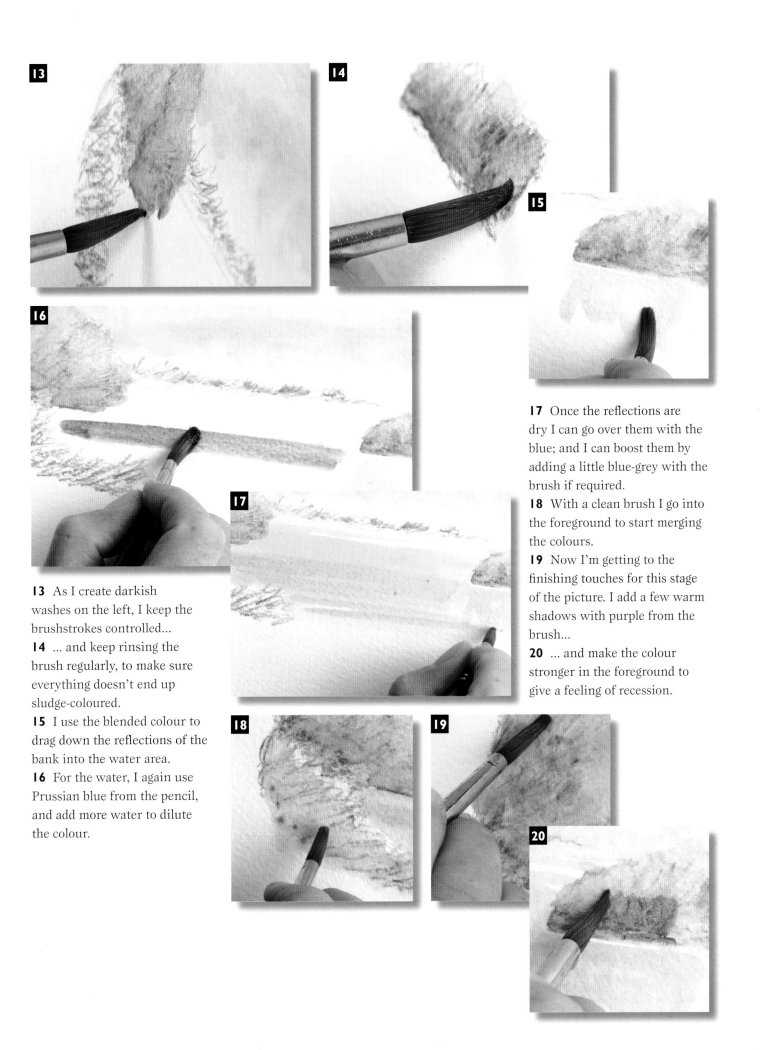

13 As I create darkish washes on the left, I keep the brushstrokes controlled...

14 ... and keep rinsing the brush regularly, to make sure everything doesn't end up sludge-coloured.

15 I use the blended colour to drag down the reflections of the bank into the water area.

16 For the water, I again use Prussian blue from the pencil, and add more water to dilute the colour.

17 Once the reflections are dry I can go over them with the blue; and I can boost them by adding a little blue-grey with the brush if required.

18 With a clean brush I go into the foreground to start merging the colours.

19 Now I'm getting to the finishing touches for this stage of the picture. I add a few warm shadows with purple from the brush...

20 ... and make the colour stronger in the foreground to give a feeling of recession.

21 I take a short break at this point, to let everything dry completely and to look at the overall picture. Working with the pencils again, I next add some squiggly lines for the foreground grass, using dark green.

22 I then repeat the strokes with blue-grey, both creating lines in new areas and going over some of the green ones.

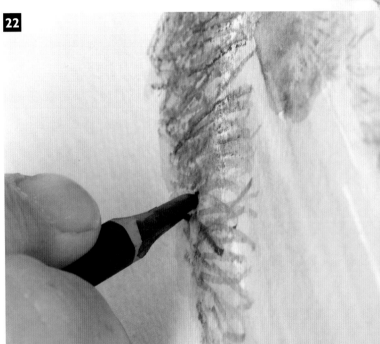

23 To repeat some of the shapes of the land in the water, I take first dark green and then blue-grey off the pencils with the brush and use this to create the darkish reflections.

24 I use the same colours on the other side of the picture, being careful to echo only the darkest shadows on the bank.

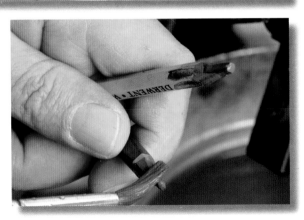

25 To match the reflections, I add a few more dark green grasses with the pencil.

26 And there we have a very simple watercolour pencil and wash painting – but I feel it needs a little more definition here and there.

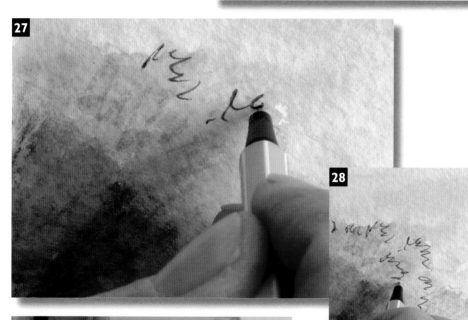

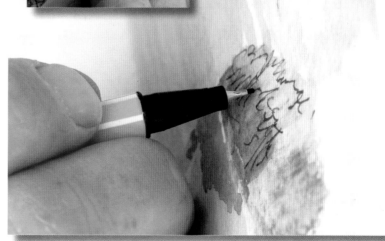

27 When everything is completely dry, I use a thin-nibbed green gel pen to add just a few squiggly lines to pull out the areas I want to stand out.

28 What I'm *not* doing here is line-and-wash work – this is purely to add a tiny, but important, amount of emphasis.

29 Moving to the right-hand bank I add a few more lines, then switch to black pen for the foreground grasses – and that's the finished painting.

EXERCISE
BUILDINGS

Unless you're planning to paint town or city scenes, your landscapes aren't likely to feature too many buildings. The quick exercises here show you how to slap on paint for a good result.

Avery simple building to make a start with is a single small cottage on moorland. The whole building can be done with just one brush.

1 Using a No. 8 round brush, paint the closest end of the building, far chimney and one sloping roof line in raw umber.
2 Make a light mix of French ultramarine blue and burnt sienna, and use this to make the two horizontal roof lines – and there's the building shape.
3 With a slightly darker blue mix, block in the roof, leaving a few white gaps.

4 While this is drying, fill in the nearest wall with a strong wash of raw umber.
5 The other visible wall is lighter than the near one, and for this use a very watery raw umber wash.
6 Now the roof is dry, make up a third, darker mix of French ultramarine and burnt sienna, and go over parts of the roof, following the slope.

7 When the light wall is dry, use a very dark mix of French ultramarine and burnt sienna and make a tick mark for the window, plus one for the ledge.
8 Finish all the windows and do the door in the same way, then use more ticks for the chimneys. A little Hooker's green and raw umber applied with a flat brush for the grass, and there's the cottage.

EXERCISE **COTTAGE**

Thatched buildings don't have sharp edges and straight lines – the character is in the unevenness, and you only need to give an impression of the thatch itself.

1 Using a gunmetal grey watercolour pencil draw a simple outline – the 'point' of the roof is actually round.
2 Use a No. 8 round brush and yellow ochre to block in the near side of the thatch, then use burnt sienna to drop in the highlighted parts of the front. Then use a black mix of French ultramarine and burnt sienna to paint the shadowed front roof.

3 With the same mix fill in the shadowed parts of the front, including the windows.
4 Now smash the brush into a watered-down mix of raw umber, splitting the hairs, and stroke it on to the dry ochre, and follow it with a watery mix of the black.
5 For the side of the barn, add more French ultramarine to the black mix with a lot of water.

6 Use the full-strength mix and a No. 3 rigger brush to paint the thatch tie across the roof, which shouldn't be a straight line.
7 For a few lines to suggest the planks at the side, use the same mix and brush.
8 To finish, go back to the round brush and a light black mix for the roof shadow. A last bit of green with the shadow of the barn, and that's it done.

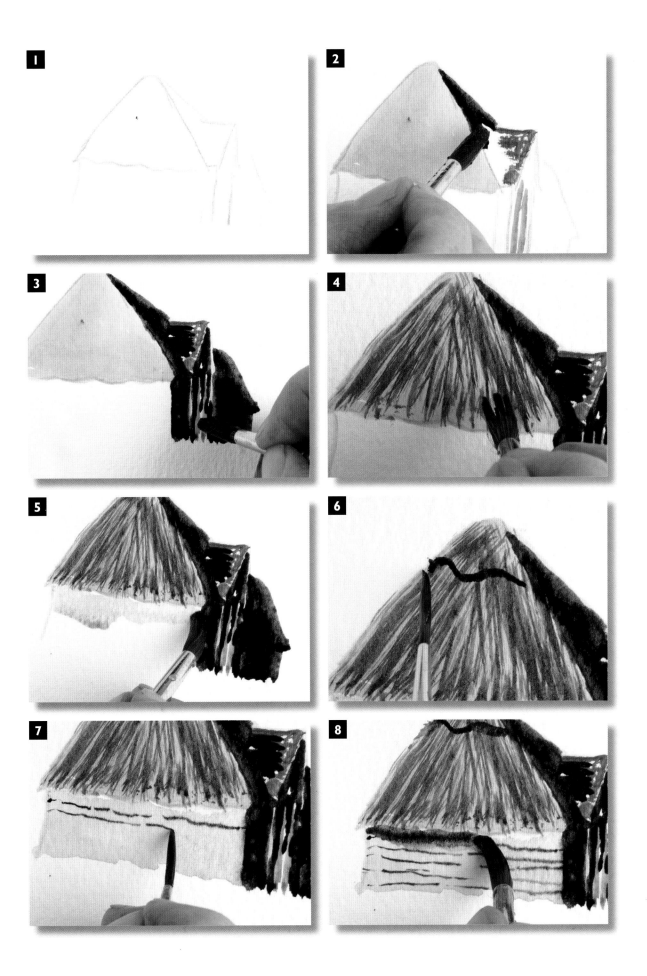

For a row or terrace of houses, the rules are the same as for the single cottage on pages 90–91, but you have to make sure the chimneys, windows and doors match up.

1 Start by drawing the end of the nearest house with a gunmetal grey pencil.

2 After extending the bottom of the roof line and adding the far wall end, draw in the chimneys, making each one smaller as it goes away. Then block in the end wall with raw umber and a No. 8 round brush.

3 Next touch in the near side of the chimney sides with the same mix.

4 Use a watered-down version of the umber for the front of the buildings, then use a light mix of Frnech ultramarine and burnt sienna for the roof slope, leaving white gaps.

5 Switching to a No. 3 rigger brush, use a black mix of French ultramarine and burnt sienna for the chimney pots, painting them with ticks.

6 As for the single cottage, use ticks to paint in the windows.

7 Then add more windows and doors, this time adding steps to the doors with a further series of ticks.

8 For the final touches, put in the television aerials and telegraph poles and wires with a light version of the roof blue, and use the same mix for the roof shadow. A bit of grass by the side, and some watered umber and blue mix in front of the houses, and you're there.

EXERCISE **ROW OF HOUSES**

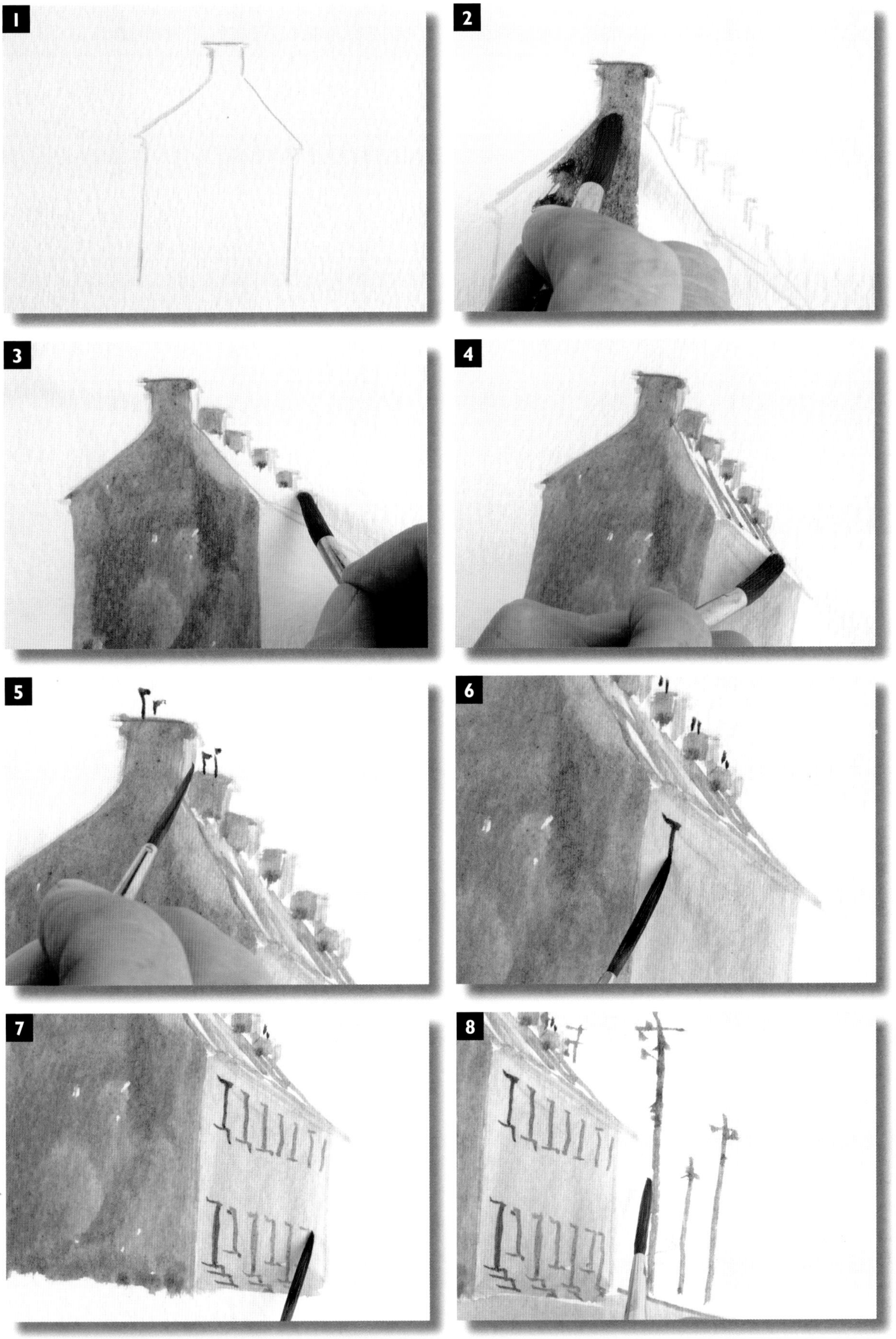

Houses and Lane

Buildings don't have to be the focal point in a picture. Here, a few houses half-hidden down a country lane are all you need.

All I have here to start with is a very simple basic outline drawing. I never use crosshatching or shading in preliminary pencil drawings because any texture or detail work should be done in the painting by the paint.

1 With a large wash I wet the sky area, then work from the top down with a watery wash of French ultramarine. I go through the tops of the trees, so that any gaps will be sky colour, not white paper.
2 I rinse and squeeze out the brush, then draw out the pigment for the clouds and let the sky dry, but not completely.

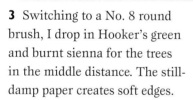

3 Switching to a No. 8 round brush, I drop in Hooker's green and burnt sienna for the trees in the middle distance. The still-damp paper creates soft edges.
4 While this is still wet, I add a watery wash of French ultramarine, mainly along the bottom, which gives a feeling of 'what's around the corner'.

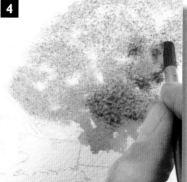

5 With a touch of raw umber I very loosely drop in the basic colour for the furthest building; at this stage I'm just blocking in, with no detail. I add a little texture to the slightly wet paper with a tiny bit of light red, and while this is drying I fill in the windows with a mix of French ultramarine and a very little burnt sienna.

6 On the nearest building I block in the shadow side of the white walls with the same mix as for the windows.

7 Working within the window frames, I use the mix for the glass panes, leaving white highlights.

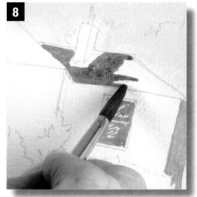

8 For the roof of the white building I use burnt sienna with a tiny touch of raw umber. Again, I don't go into detail and leave a few smidgens of white. I then paint the shadow side the same colour as the side of the building.

9 While this is drying, I move back to the furthest building – which means that I get on with the painting more quickly than if I were to use a hairdryer to dry one part. I use the roof mix from step 8 to add the roof line.

10 For the roof of the barn on the left I use a slightly darker version of the burnt sienna and raw umber mix of the other roofs. As always, I make sure to leave some white – if I need white, there's no finer white than that of the paper.

11 For the windows of the barn I use a darker version of the French ultramarine and burnt sienna mix I used on the other buildings.

12 I make up a very watered wash of raw umber for the barn walls, painting this into the tree shapes.

13 Where the main barn wall goes into shadow, I add a touch of French ultramarine to the raw umber to darken it slightly.

14 While the paint on the barn wall dries, I move back to the furthest building and colour in the shadow side of the garden wall with the raw umber and French ultramarine mix, making sure it gets weaker the further into the distance it goes.

15 I bring this colour all the way along the wall, and then dilute the mix to go round the corner to the front-facing part of the wall in front of the white building.

16 Adding some burnt sienna into the wall mix, I put some stones into the barn wall – just a few strokes, as I'm painting the wall, not building it.

17 To get a slightly darker tone, I add a touch of French ultramarine into the mix.

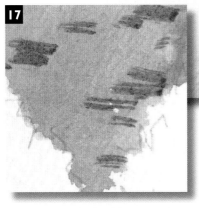

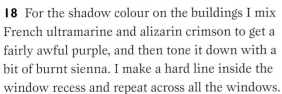

18 For the shadow colour on the buildings I mix French ultramarine and alizarin crimson to get a fairly awful purple, and then tone it down with a bit of burnt sienna. I make a hard line inside the window recess and repeat across all the windows.

19 Using the same mix I add a strong shadow line where the roof of the barn meets the wall, toning this down with a clean damp brush.

20 I then put in a few touches of the shadow mix along the barn roof – for a big, solid roof such as this, I need to make quite wide marks.

21 After adding quite a bit of water to the shadow mix I apply it lightly to show the shadows of the foliage on the front of the white building.

22 I then add some shadows to fill in the gaps on the furthest building, down the gate and on the chimneys, using the same watery mix.

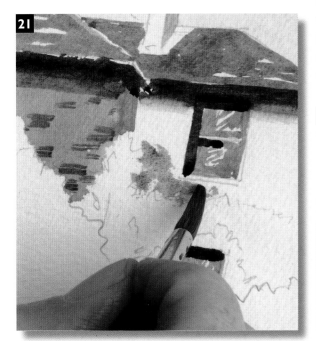

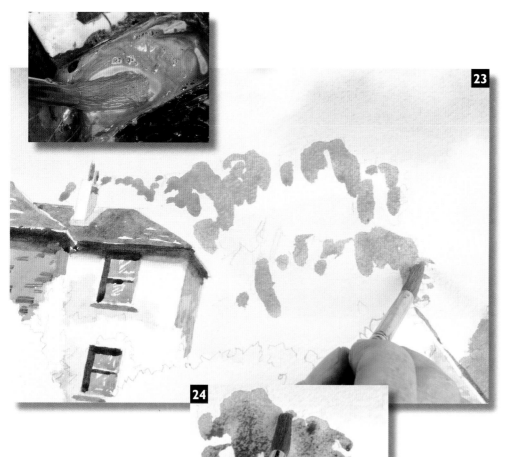

23 Once again while everything is drying, I move on to another part of the painting. For the big trees behind the buildings, I start with a well watered wash of yellow ochre for the top part.

24 I make a light mix of Hooker's green and burnt sienna and go over most of the first wash, remembering to leave a few gaps of the sky colour through the foliage.

25 Still keeping an eye on the gaps in the trees, I apply a mix of raw umber and French ultramarine to show a few boughs; even though the main trunk is hidden from view, the branches must be believable and not look as if they're hanging in thin air.

26 Where the foliage comes down to meet the buildings I add some French ultramarine to the green mix – this makes the buildings zing out of the background. I merge the colours together with the side of the brush while they are still damp.

27 For the ivy growing up the buildings I split the hairs of the round brush and dab yellow ochre on to the paper, not atempting to paint each and every leaf.

28 Over this I put a nice strong mix of Hooker's green and burnt sienna, again splitting the hairs and dabbing the colour on.

29 Even ivy is going to cast a shadow, so I go back to the basic shadow mix of French ultramarine, alizarin crimson and burnt sienna and stipple it over the other washes with split hairs.

30 I repeat steps 27, 28 and 29 for the ivy on the furthest building, using the same technique and weaker versions of each of the mixes to give the impression of greater distance. The technical term for this is 'tonal recession'.

31 With the shadow mix I cast a little shadow from the chimney on to the roof of the white building.

32 I then use a much stronger version to darken the bases of some of the trees.

33 As this dries, I return to yellow ochre to dab a first wash on to the foreground bushes.

34 Still leaving some white gaps, I stipple a mix of Hooker's green and light red over the first ochre wash.

35 Once again I go in with the shadow colour on the wet washes, keeping this colour darkest in the gateway to the building in the distance.

HOUSES AND LANE

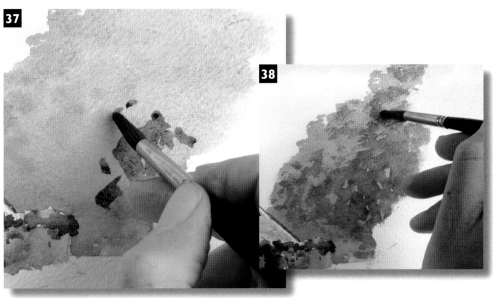

36 I add a few strokes of a raw umber, French ultramarine and burnt sienna mix for the stones in the garden wall, not trying to add detail but a bit of texture.

37 While this is drying, I go back to the trees in the distance and apply a mix of Hooker's green and French ultramarine to bring in some texture and contours.

38 I then strengthen the mix and add a few shadows among the mass of foliage.

39 I use the same mix as in step 37 to block in the bush in front of the barn, still leaving some gaps and cutting in front of the ivy on the buildings. Again I strengthen the mix to add variety and texture.

40 Where the bush is darkest I add some of the shadow mix, being careful to cut in around the white fence as a negative shape, rather than using masking fluid.

41 I fill in the gaps in the near gateway with a little light red on the steps and inner path, and then mix this with raw umber and plenty of water for the main path.

42 Changing to a ¾ in flat wash brush, I use the same watery mix to pick up the surface of the paper for the main track of the lane, keeping the colour lighter further away. I then let everything dry completely.

43 To start the grass verges, I apply yellow ochre with the flat wash brush.

44 While this is wet, I dab on a mix of Hooker's green, burnt sienna and a touch of French ultramarine.

45 I tap with the corner of the brush in the furthest bits of the verges, leaving some white.

46 While this is drying, I move to the right-hand trees, using the side of the wash brush to tap on some yellow ochre.

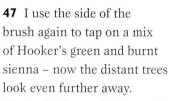

47 I use the side of the brush again to tap on a mix of Hooker's green and burnt sienna – now the distant trees look even further away.

48 At the front of the trees I use yellow ochre with a bit of alizarin crimson.

49 While this is wet I stipple on a mix of Hooker's green, French ultramarine and burnt sienna, splitting the brush hairs and allowing some background to show through. I then add some French ultramarine to darken the trees.

50 I leave the trees and start the right foreground verge with yellow ochre.

Top Tip

IF YOU DON'T LEAVE GAPS IN TREES AND BUSHES, THE BIRDS CAN'T FLY INTO OR THROUGH THEM!

HOUSES AND LANE

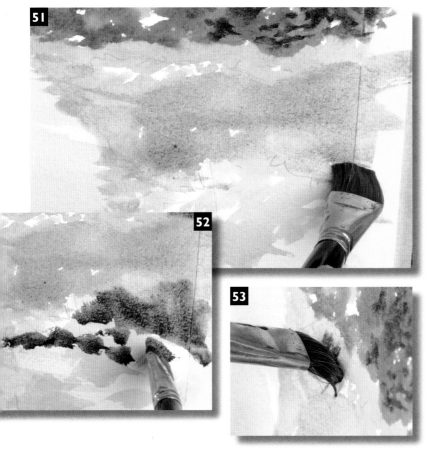

51 I splash a daub of a raw umber and light red mix from the track into the right-hand edge.
52 For a rich, dark green I apply a mix of Hooker's green, burnt sienna and French ultramarine over the wet washes.
53 I flick and dab the green mix to show the rough patches of grass, allowing some of the original ochre wash to show through.

54 While this dries, I return to the left-hand verge with the shadow mix, using the side of the wash brush to bring the shadows down the verges to the lane.
55 I switch to the No. 8 round brush to put the shadow mix along the white fence posts and a very diluted version along the rails. I then add the shadows to the right-hand verge.
56 To tie the painting together, I apply a very diluted dark wash of the shadow mix across the lane from the verge.
57 I block in these shadows, add shadow lines to the steps with a light mix of shadow colours, and allow everything to dry. I then remove the tape for a crisply framed finished painting.

C.M. EVANS. 04

Castle and Estuary

After the quiet country lane in the last project,

I decided to go for something grander: this is

Warkworth Castle in Northumberland.

In this view, from the River Coquet, there's quite a lot of detail. I didn't try to draw it all, but focused on getting the castle fairly true to life; after that I just picked out some of the prominent and large buildings, and then stuck in a few rooftops and chimneys for a general impression. Working outdoors, the only race is to get the sky down on paper – after that you can relax, enjoy yourself, look at the view around you and soak up the atmosphere.

1 With a large flat wash brush I wet the entire sky area. I then use the brush to mix together a little yellow ochre and burnt sienna, and put it on to the bottom of the areas and bring it upwards. While this is still wet I add some touches of French ultramarine above it.

2 Still with the sky area wet, I mix French ultramarine and light red for the outer blue areas at each side. As always with skies, I work quickly into the wet paper and washes.

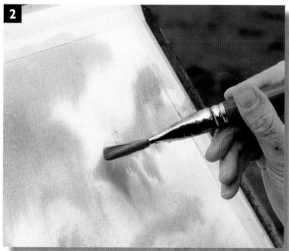

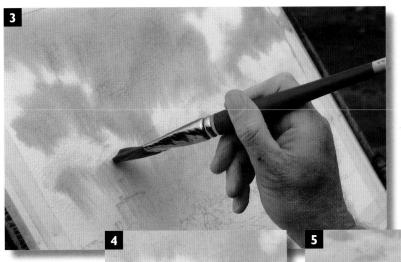

3 I rinse and squeeze the brush, then use it to draw out the pigment along the bottom edge of the sky area and into the sky to create clouds.

4 For the darker patches beneath the clouds, I use the French ultramarine and light red mix. So far, this has taken under five minutes.

5 As the sky dries, the first mix begins to come to the fore and creates a glow among the clouds; this will have an influence on the rest of the picture.

6 Now I move to the landscape in the far distance. Switching to a No. 8 round brush, I make up a weak mix of French ultramarine and light red and drop this in for the trees on the horizon, which look like a few lumpy bits.

7 Below these I put on a little bit of well-watered yellow ochre and stroke the pigment down – I don't make horizontal or vertical strokes for hills, but follow the actual contours.

8 For the trees and bushes here I use a mix of yellow ochre and a tiny hint of Hooker's green.

Castle and Estuary **111**

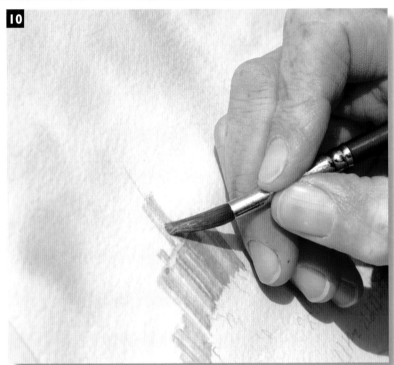

9 To start the castle I make up a mix of raw umber and yellow ochre. The light is coming from the left, so I use this mix for the darker parts on the right – these shadows create the true form.

10 I then put straight yellow ochre on to the sunlit parts while the shadowed sides are still wet.

11 For the church spire and tower in the town I use the raw umber and yellow ochre mix.

12 Next I add a little French ultramarine to the mix for the shadow side of the spire and the church roof.

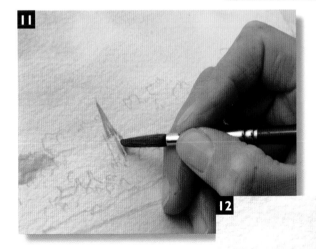

13 With a darkish but watery mix of Hooker's green and French ultramarine I drop in some of the distant trees by the castle.

14 While this wash is still wet, I add a mix of Hooker's green and burnt sienna and merge this in from below.

15 I then bring the mixes in from the right across the front of the castle, cutting into the building carefully. Here and there I add a few touches of yellow ochre to merge with the darker colours.

16 To soften the base of the general mêlée of trees here, I use a fairly weak wash of French ultramarine.

17 I apply a light wash of Hooker's green and yellow ochre for the hillside on which the castle is standing.

18 For the darker greens going into the houses and filling in the tree areas across the church and over to the right, I use a mix of Hooker's green and burnt sienna.

19 While the tree washes are drying I make up my shadow colour mix of French ultramarine, alizarin crimson and burnt sienna – you should know this recipe by heart now! – and put the very darkest shadow areas on the castle.

20 I have a look at which parts will cast shadows on to adjacent areas of the castle, especially the castellation to the left of the main building. I put in very light verticals for windows.

21 Before my hand gets too cold to hold the No. 3 rigger, I use this brush to add the smallest details without trying to be too exact at this distance. I use French ultramarine, burnt sienna and alizarin crimson for the flagpole, and a straight wash of alizarin crimson for the flag itself. You can see how windy it is in the photo below – and that the clouds have now covered the sky, which is why you need to get skies down quickly.

CASTLE AND ESTUARY

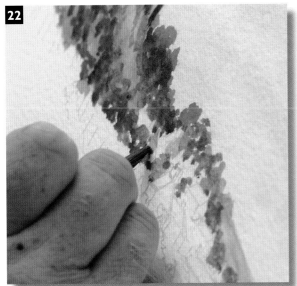

22 Switching back to the round brush, I use a light wash of raw umber to block in some of the buildings among the foliage.

23 I use a darker wash of raw umber for the shadow side of some of the buildings; this brightens up the light side.

24 For most of the rooftops across the whole picture I use a wash of burnt sienna, and then make a contrasting mix of French ultramarine and burnt sienna for the remaining roofs. I use this mix to fill in the shadows among the trees by the church.

25 Moving to the nearest buildings, I use a very watery wash of raw umber for the brighter side, and French ultramarine and burnt sienna for the sides that are in shadow.

26 With the rigger brush, I use my shadow colour to put in just the impression of a few windows in the houses, then switch back to the round brush for some bits of roof shadow.

27 To put the darker trees over the lighter dry washes around the church and above the town I use a mix of Hooker's green, burnt sienna and French ultramarine.

28 I then put a diluted version of this mix along the bottom of the buildings.

29 For the light strand below the buildings I apply a wash of yellow ochre with a ¾in flat wash brush.

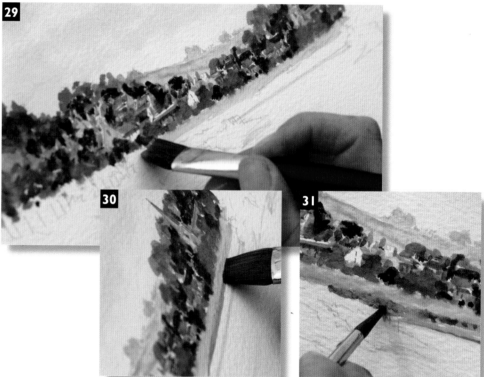

CASTLE AND ESTUARY

30 Using the same brush I then go below this line with a light mix of Hooker's green and burnt sienna to make an even thinner line...

31 ...and below this I switch back to the round brush to apply the green mix with some French ultramarine in it.

32 Going back to the area below the castle, I start by cutting into the green with the flat brush and a wash of yellow ochre.

33 With the ¾in flat wash brush I bring down the yellow ochre while it is still wet.

34 I then go into this with a mix of Hooker's green and burnt sienna, leaving some patches of white paper.

35 Back with the flat brush I continue to bring the green down, just making a few marks and not attempting to block in the colour.

36 Even when I bring down the green to the foreground, I take care not to make the shade a solid one.

37 I switch back to the round brush and a stronger version of the green mix for the bushes.

38 For the smallest marks here I use the side of the brush as well as the tip.

39 Using the shadow mix of French ultramarine, alizarin crimson and burnt sienna, I add more darks among the bushes and create contours and shadow areas among the grasses, going down to the river bank.

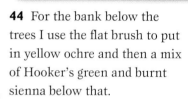

40 With an almost black mix of French ultramarine and burnt sienna and using the rigger brush, I add the fence posts, getting smaller in the distance.

41 I start the trees on the right with the flat brush, tapping yellow ochre on to the paper.

42 While this is wet, I tap on a mix of Hooker's green and burnt sienna to give a ragged edge.

43 Back with the round brush I drop in a watery mix of French ultramarine and burnt sienna so that it merges with the first two washes.

44 For the bank below the trees I use the flat brush to put in yellow ochre and then a mix of Hooker's green and burnt sienna below that.

45 I then add a mix of raw umber and French ultramarine for the muddy shore, merging this into the bank washes.

46 After wetting all the river area, I put in a wash of Hooker's green and burnt sienna for the reflections of the trees.

47 I then put in quite a strong mix of French ultramarine and burnt sienna for the ripples on the right by the bank.

CASTLE AND ESTUARY

48 Just as with the sky, I aim to have the river area finished within no more than three or four minutes. I start by brushing on a watery mix of French ultramarine and a tiny bit of light red, merging this in softly with the other washes in the river.

49 I rinse and squeeze out the flat brush and draw out the paint in horizontal bands to show the highlights in the water and create some movement. It's important not to overdo this – if each strip cost £5 to take out, how many would you remove?

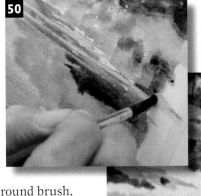

50 Using my shadow mix and the round brush, I add a little shadow beneath the right-hand bank, and then do the same for the left-hand bank in the foreground.

51 Finally I go back to the flat wash brush and use a mix of raw umber and yellow ochre to give the impression of a muddy stretch going down to the water on the left. I stroke on the watery wash horizontally, taking care not to dull the highlights.

Et voilà! My big outdoor adventure is finished, and even if the sky has cleared up, it's time to pack up quickly and find a nice warm café to have a cup of tea and thaw out my fingers.

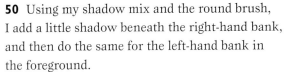

Index

Entries in **bold** refer to projects

Branch	Date
DW	1/06